Netherlands

Editor Susan Ward
Design Patrick Frean
Picture Research Frances Middlestorb
                      Mary Walsh
Production Vivienne Driscoll
Consultant Arthur Eperon
Illustrations Ron Hayward Associates
                  John Shackell
                  Patrick Frean
Maps Matthews and Taylor Associates

Cover: A harvest of gold. These lovely blossoms are only a means to an end. The real profit lies in something far less attractive—the dirt-caked bulb. *Popper*

Endpaper: Two children take their ease on one of the country's many canals. The windmills in the background form what is probably the most popular image of the country. In fact, of 947 windmills in the Netherlands, only some 300 are still working. *Nationaal Foto Persbureau.*

Page 6: A cyclist pursues his solitary way over a stone bridge in Amsterdam. The chestnut trees and lazy canals of the capital city provide a serene contrast to the bustle and verve of one of Europe's busiest commercial centres. *Dennis Moore.*

Photographic sources Key to positions of illustrations: *(T)* top, *(C)* centre, *(B)* bottom, *(L)* left, *(R)* right. Actualit: *22(TL), 42(BL), 50(T)* Ampfoto, Amsterdam: *23(BR)* Atlas van Stolk: *26/27(B), 42/43(C), 48(BR), 49(TL)* Camera Press: *22/23(C)* J. Alan Cash: *15(BR), 21(BR), 23(BC), 27(TL), 30(BL), 35(TR), 39(TL) (TR), 40(TL) (BL), 43(TL), 47(BR), 52(BL)* Cas Oothuys: *21(TR)* Colour Library International: *35(BR), 51(BL)* Concertgebouw Orchestra: *40/41(B)* Cooper-Bridgeman Library: *24/25(T)* Mary Evans Picture Library: *26(BL)* Robert Harding Associates: *31(TR), 34(BR)* Haags Gemeentemuseum, The Hague: *25(TR)* Het Nederlandsch Persmuseum: *45(TL)* Hilversam TV Studios: *44/45(C)* Keystone: *11(BR), 28/29(B)* Madurodam: *41(TR)* Mansell Collection: *13(TR), 20(BL), 21(TL), 23(TR), 51(TL)* Berten van Manen: *19(BR), 53(TL)* March-Penny (Peter Sackett): *8(T), 17(BR)* Dennis Moore: *10(BL) (BR), 12(BR), 14(B), 15(BL) (R), 16(TL), 18(TL) (BL), 19(TL) (TR), 24(BR), 30(BR), 31(TL) (BL) (BR), 33(CR) (BR), 38(BL), 39(BR), 42(TC), 43(TR), 44(BC) (T), 46(BC), 47(TR), 49(TR), 52/53(B), 49(BL)* National Gallery, London: *24(BL), 25(BL)* National Maritime Museum, Greenwich: *20/21(B)* Netherlands National Oorlogsmuseum: *21(BC)* Netherlands National Tourist Office: *9(C) (B), 11(BL), 13(TC), 32(TC), 33(BR), 36(BR), 37(TR), 45(BL)* Picturepoint: *34(BL)* Rijksmuseum van Ouden: *9(C)* Rijksolken Diest: *37(TL)* Royal Netherlands Embassy: *10(TL), 15(TL), 36(BL), 37(BL), 43(BR)* SEF: *27(BR)* Spectrum: *16(BR)* Volvo, Eindhoven: *38(TL)* VVV Limburg: *41(BR)* ZEFA: *10(TC) (TR), 12(BL), 17(TR) (BL), 25(BR), 35(BL), 37(BR).*

First published 1976
Macdonald Educational
Holywell House, Worship Street
London E.C.2

ISBN 0 356 05272 9
Published in the United States by Silver Burdett Company, Morristown, N. J. 1977 Printing

Library of Congress Catalog Card No. 77-70193

2 127/78 Rehers Toylr 7.96

Netherlands

the land and its people

Frank E. Huggett

Macdonald Educational

Contents

8 The making of the Netherlands
10 Water—friend and ancient foe
12 The Dutch influence
14 Family life
16 A foundation of faith
18 Education
20 A history of resistance
22 A passion for peace
24 Patron of the arts
26 Merchants and seamen
28 Sports and sportsmen
30 Shops and shopping
32 Eating the Dutch way
34 Amsterdam—Venice of the North
36 Monarchy and the Hague
38 Farms and factories
40 Time off
42 Waterways and bicycles
44 Media and communication
46 Customs and costumes
48 Heroes in fact and fiction
50 A sturdy independence
52 A progressive society
54 Reference: Geography and Government
56 Reference: History and the Arts
58 Reference: the Economy
60 Gazetteer
61 Index
62 Political map of the Netherlands
63 Physical map of the Netherlands

The making of the Netherlands

► Despite the fact that the Netherlands is such a small country —about one-and-a-half times as big as Wales— it is a land of variety and contrasts. Though it is based on water, not all of it is flat and guarded by windmills. In the south, below the estuaries of the three great European rivers of the Rhine, the Maas and the Scheldt, there is some delightful wooded, hilly country in Limburg and North Brabant. The necessities of trade have long made most people live in the trading seaports and cities in the west.

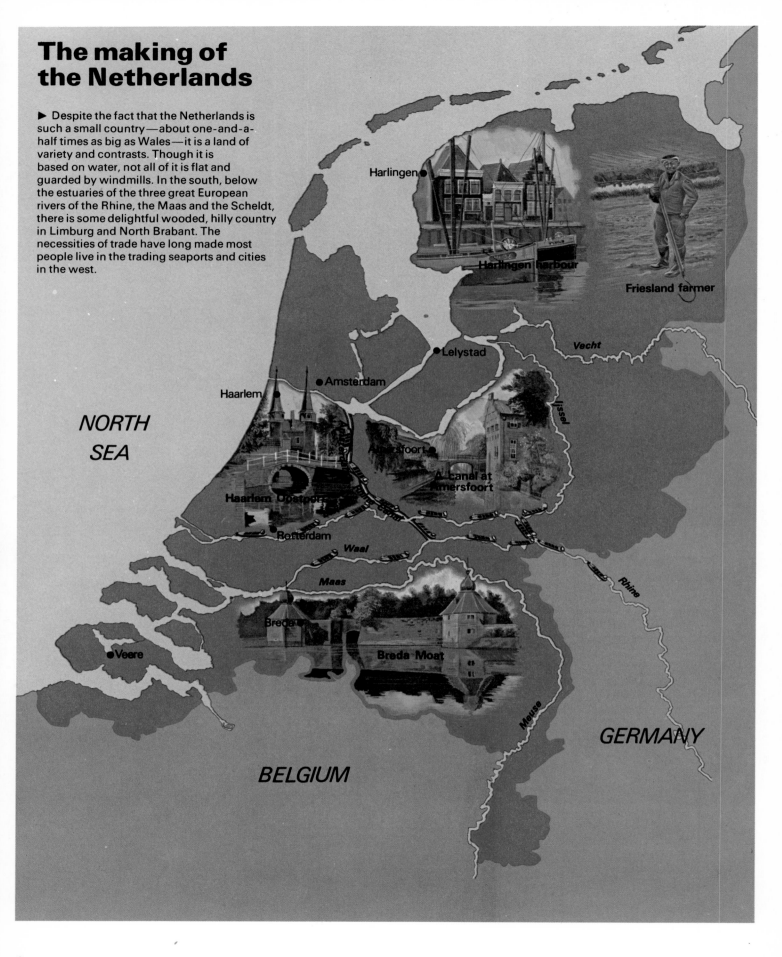

Harlingen

Harlingen harbour

Friesland farmer

Lelystad

Vecht

Amsterdam

Haarlem

NORTH SEA

IJssel

Amersfoort

A canal at Amersfoort

Haarlem Oostpoort

Rotterdam

Waal

Maas

Rhine

Breda

Breda Moat

Veere

Meuse

GERMANY

BELGIUM

A history of change

The Netherlands has been repeatedly invaded—by man and water. In prehistoric times, tribes from central and southern Europe came down the great rivers or across the vast European plain to settle. Much later, the armies of more powerful neighbours made the country one of the main battlefields of Europe. The North Sea has frequently swept through the shifting line of sand dunes on the coast, to form, at one point, the Zuider Zee. And the three great rivers, which gouge out their estuaries in Zeeland and South Holland, have often burst their banks.

The country has always been in a state of flux. Its size and frontiers have changed many times. In the Middle Ages, it was linked with neighbouring feudal principalities to form a Burgundian kingdom. Spain, France and Germany are all former rulers.

These invasions have helped to give a sense of national unity, despite differences in religion, topography and economy between the eleven provinces. The most importantly historically has been Holland, which is now divided into two. It has given the whole country its second name.

▲ Over two thousand years ago, settlers built mounds of earth where their cattle could take refuge from the daily floods in the coastal regions.

▲ This oak carving, dating from about 4,400 B.C., was found in the estuary of the river Maas near Willemstad. It is one of the earliest depictions of the human face in northwest Europe.

◀ Traditions die hard in the countryside. Saxon-style farmhouses, with steep, overhanging thatched roofs, are still a characteristic feature of Friesland.

Water—friend and ancient foe

The battle

The Dutch have a special right to feel proud of their small, low-lying country, for without their indomitable persistence and courage about a half of it would still be under water. Throughout the centuries they have been waging an unending battle against the incursions of the North Sea and the flooding of the three great rivers, the Rhine, the Maas and the Scheldt.

The first sea dykes were built by the Frisians, using wicker baskets, sleds and their bare hands. From the fifteenth century windmills were used to drain the lakes and marshes. Although there are still nearly 1,000 windmills, very few of them are used nowadays. Huge pumping stations work day and night to flush surplus water through the network of canals into the sea.

And the spoils

In this battle against the waters, victory has gone first to one side and then to the other. The Dutch have lost about 566,580 hectares (14m. acres) of land and gained about 687,900 hectares (17m. acres) in the last eight centuries. Their greatest victory has been the draining of the Zuider Zee which is due to be completed by 1980.

Although water has been such a relentless enemy, it has also been the country's greatest friend. Her rivers and easy access to the Baltic and the North Sea have made the Netherlands a hub of European trade since the early seventeenth century.

Traditional drainage system

▲ Jan Adriaanszoon Leeghwater (1575-1650) planned to drain the 40,000-acre Haarlem lake with 160 windmills. The scheme was not completed until the nineteenth century.

▲ Only a few windmills still keep their sails turning. Modern pumping stations keep the feet of Dutchmen dry.

◄ Sheep may safely graze on these protective dikes. The land-starved Dutch do not waste any patch of soil.

▼ In the old days windmills were often used in a series to pump water out of the low-lying land into a ring canal, where it drained away into the sea. There are still nearly 1,000 windmills in the country, but very few of them are now in use.

▲ *Before:* the creation of a polder. Water is pumped away to reveal a vast expanse of mud and puddles where reeds grow. Birds and small animals soon make it their home.

▲ *After:* grass is sown and houses built on the reclaimed land. The rich soil makes excellent pastures for cattle. The Dutch try to avoid a "checkerboard" landscape.

◀ Tree-lined canals, above the level of the land, carry surplus water to the sea.

▼ The last great floods in 1953 caused the loss of 1,835 lives. This scene of devastation in Stellendam was repeated in countless villages in Zeeland and South Holland.

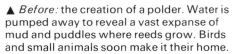

The Dutch influence

▲ Dutch advances in retailing have brought benefits to shoppers in many other European countries in modern times.

Water power

Dutch influence was at its peak in the seventeenth century. The success of this small nation of only two million people in defying and eventually defeating Spain, the greatest imperial power of the age, made it 'the wonder of all Europe'.

Dutch ships were the envy of the world. Peter the Great, the Tsar, was so greatly impressed that he made a special visit to the Netherlands to work in Dutch shipyards as a labourer so that he could learn their skills. Yachting, which was popularized by Charles II of England, originated in the Netherlands. When Charles returned from exile, the Dutch presented him with a yacht which became the prototype for later English models.

Exploration and innovation

Dutch explorers and seamen sailed to the far corners of the world. At one time, the Dutch flag flew in five continents. They brought back many exotic plants and flowers, from the East and from South Africa, which still grace European gardens.

The services of their hydraulic engineers were in demand throughout Europe for dredging, draining and reclaiming land. They created many fertile stretches of land out of bogs and marshes. The Fens in East Anglia is just one example. Meanwhile, Dutch painters, engravers and craftsmen were at work in many European courts.

Foreign visitors flocked into the Netherlands to admire the scrupulously clean houses and the neatly planned towns. The sliding sash window, the wing-back chair and the ornate cabinets on stands were copied in many other countries, particularly in Britain. Typical baroque architecture, a marriage of curlicue gables steep roofs and shuttered windows, made its way to the far corners of the earth. A Dutchman invented the first effective pendulum clock from which the long-case, or grandfather, clock was developed.

The Dutch created the first bourgeois society in the world. Many of its features—the passion for cleanliness, the concern for social justice, the emphasis on domesticity—have had an enduring influence.

▲ Only the signpost, exotic flora, and shop signs show that this corner of Willemstad in Curaçao is not in the Netherlands. The Dutch took this Caribbean island in 1634.

▶ Tulips were originally introduced into Europe from Turkey in the sixteenth century. Dutch skill in cultivating these exotic flowers have made them popular world-wide.

Three great inventors

Simon Stevin (1584-1620), the mathematician, made important advances in navigation and pioneered the use of the decimal system.

Antony van Leeuwenhoek (1632-1723) made many discoveries under his microscope, including the red blood corpuscles.

Christiaan Huygens (1629-1695) invented the pendulum clock, improved the telescope and made astronomical discoveries.

▲ Exquisite blue-and-white glazed tiles have been made in the Netherlands since the seventeenth century. Early tiles depict musketry drill, flowers, ships and animals. Many of them show a marked oriental influence, derived from Chinese porcelain.

▼ The Boers have played a major part in South African history ever since Jan van Riebeeck established a settlement at the Cape of Good Hope in 1652. These sturdy pioneers with their Calvinist spirit of independence pushed the frontiers north against great odds.

The Dutch connection

Dutch treat

Dutch uncle

Double Dutch

▲ There are nearly thirty expressions using the word "Dutch" in the English language. Most are uncomplimentary. Many originated in the seventeenth century when the Dutch and English fought each other three times.

Family life

A home-loving nation

Regardless of whether it's a modern flat, a couple of rooms in an old terrace house or a barge moored on a canal, a Dutchman's home is his castle. The Dutch like their homes to be as clean, comfortable and cosy —or *gezellig*—as possible. That is why on average they spend more than any other national of the E.E.C. on furniture and household goods. For the same reasons, far fewer married women with children go out to work, though with inflation and rising standards of living that is beginning to change.

The family occupies a special place in Dutch life. There is nothing most Dutchmen like better than having a quiet evening at home with their family, watching the television, reading a book or the newspaper, or just discussing the events of the day.

Generous but overcrowded

There are two words to describe the family : *gezin*, the immediate relatives, and *familie*, the wider circle. In the Netherlands neither is neglected. Visits are frequent ; letters are written regularly ; and the birthdays of all are celebrated. Some doctors have even identified a new malady—family sickness— which overcomes those who are too conscious of their obligations.

Land shortage has always created housing problems in the Netherlands. These have become acute since the end of the war, particularly in the over-crowded western region. Since 1945 over two million homes have been built, including many flats which, however, have not always satisfied their occupants. Lack of space and privacy, and noise, have been the biggest complaints.

Although the Dutch are such a home-loving people, relatively few own their own houses.

▲ The Dutch get up early and many of them, particularly in the big cities, go to bed quite late. After an active day at work, they often spend a relaxing evening reading and playing games.

▼ From the air it may look like a housing estate, but these are merely allotments— popular all over Holland. The thrifty Dutch live in these "sheds" in summer and let their houses.

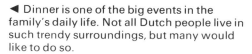

▲ Quiet corners of towns and cities, like this one in Amsterdam, become psychedelic playgrounds. Little paddling pools are used as children's ice rinks in the winter.

◄ Dinner is one of the big events in the family's daily life. Not all Dutch people live in such trendy surroundings, but many would like to do so.

► The Dutch can make a home anywhere, even on a barge at Haarlem. Net curtains go up at the window, and the washing flies proudly from the mast. There's often a garden on deck, too.

A foundation of faith

▲ Divisions between the Catholic south and the Protestant north are now less marked, but there are still distinguishing features. One is the pre-Lenten carnival which is celebrated mainly in Limburg and North Brabant. For three whole days and nights, these two southern provinces are given over to merry-making and enjoyment.

▲ A Dutch Reformed Church at Den Oever with a painted wooden tower. Protestant churches are usually opened only when services are being held.

One God, many sects

It has been said that if you put one Dutchman down on a desert island he would only pray; but if you put two or three together there would soon be as many different sects. The Dutch are devout, but also independent in their views, which helps to explain the large number of churches and the recent disputes between the Catholic hierarchy and Rome.

Religion has always played a key role in Dutch history. It was one of the major factors in the revolt against Catholic Spain in the seventeenth century. During the long struggle, the Calvinist church became the recognized, though not established, church. But many Catholics continued to live happily in the big cities and there were an even greater number in the southern provinces captured from Spain. By the late eighteenth century, it is estimated that one-third of the population was Catholic.

A Catholic majority

Catholic emancipation was granted in 1853, but discrimination continued in jobs, education and the public service. The disputes between the Catholics, Protestants

▼ The strict Calvinist village of Staphorst is a living museum where old customs and traditions are still maintained as part of an active faith.

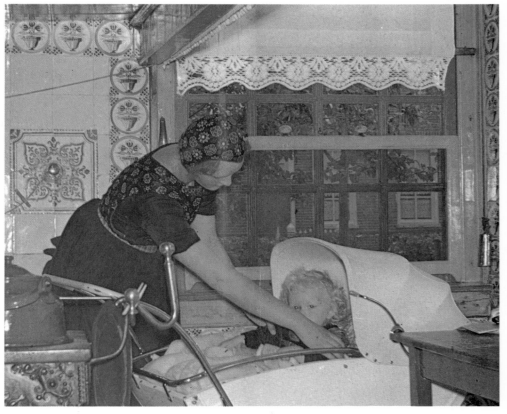

and the secular Liberals and Socialists gradually created a divided nation. They organised their own political parties, trade unions, schools, universities, radio stations, libraries, health services—even football leagues. Society became divided into three or four different blocs—*verzuiling*, as the Dutch call it.

Since 1960 the Catholics have become the biggest group, which has enabled them to feel more independent of Rome. They have become one of the most progressive churches in Europe. Over 300 priests have left to get married; ritual has been altered; and one church is now a hippy bazaar.

On the Protestant side there are two main Calvinist churches and a profusion of smaller sects, about twenty in all. Some still uphold ancient beliefs in the will of God, refusing inoculation and insurance.

But, as in other countries, the Churches are beginning to lose their hold, particularly among the young. Over twenty per-cent of the population are now classified as 'non-churchly' and there is a growing ecumenical movement. Strangely, the only legal form of marriage is civil, though many couples have a church ceremony, too.

▲ A wedding at Volendam, just north of Amsterdam, where the traditional and the modish create an unusual mixture of styles.

◀ St. Nicholas Abbey in Middelburg, Zeeland. Secularised during the Eighty Years' War, it is now the seat of provincial government.

▼ A sister from the beguinage at Breda. Other nuns have moved with the times. One recently became a member of the city council in The Hague.

Education

Religion and the three R's

One unique feature of the Dutch educational system is the high proportion of denominational schools. Since the First World War they have been given exactly the same grants and subsidies as state and municipal schools, which provide a 'neutral' education. As a result some 70 per cent of children at primary level and 60 per cent at secondary level attend denominational or private schools.

Although this satisfies the desire for freedom in education, it produces some wasteful triplication, particularly in small towns and villages.

Compulsory education lasts from the ages of six to sixteen, but nursery schools are provided nationwide for younger children. Although attendance is voluntary, they cater for 95 per cent of the five-year-olds.

◀ New schools have modern equipment, but the desks often continue to be arranged in a formal manner.

▼ Self-expression is encouraged in primary schools through many craft and artistic activities, including embroidery and knitting.

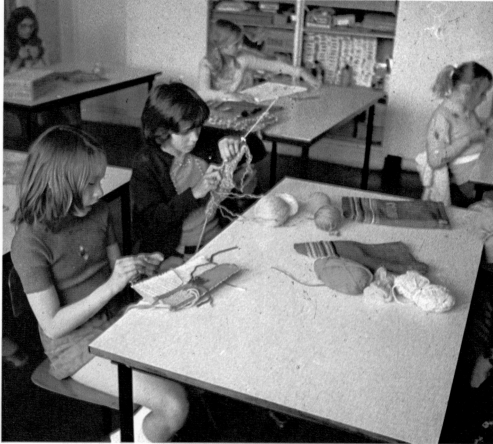

A move toward reform

In the last decade the whole educational system has been in a state of transition and reform. Pupils have been given a much bigger freedom of choice in the subjects they study. An initial transitional, or bridge, year has been introduced in which the child can display and examine its own potentialities. Although provision has been made for comprehensive schools—*scholengemeenschappen*—very few have been opened. Many educationists favour extended courses in a middle school.

The reduction in subjects studied at secondary level has increased the number of applicants for university places. At the same time, shortage of money has resulted in a virtual freeze on the number of students. In 1974 the Dutch tried to solve the problem by introducing a ballot for university places.

Education in the Netherlands

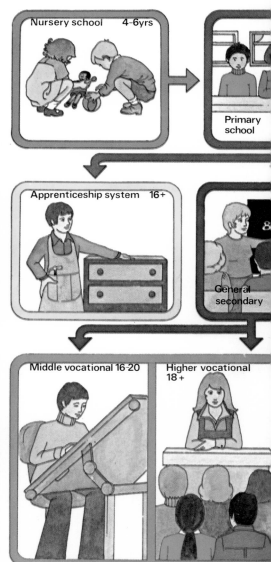

Nursery school 4-6yrs

Primary school

Apprenticeship system 16+

General secondary

Middle vocational 16-20

Higher vocational 18+

◄ Chalk and talk has less place now in secondary education. Pupils are taken out of school to explore the city around them. These students are having the workings of the canal system explained to them.

▶ The colourful graduation ceremony at Leiden University, founded in 1575, the oldest university in the country.

▼ Vocational schools are a strong feature of the educational system. Many other practical subjects are taught in addition to bakery, such as shop-keeping and house-painting.

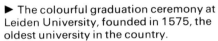

Lower vocational 12+

6-12 yrs

Pre-university 12-18

12-18

Art school

University 18+

A history of resistance

▼ Philip II of Spain put a price on the head of William the Silent. He was assassinated on July 10, 1584, at his Delft home, by a Burgundian, Balthasar Gérard.

Freedom from the Spanish yoke

As a small nation in a highly important strategic position, the Dutch have had to fight many battles both on land and at sea to retain their freedom.

The nation's shape was hammered out on the anvil of the Eighty Years' War against Spain, one of the most prolonged, complex and bloody struggles in history. The fighting line moved remorselessly back and forth across the rivers, fields and dykes, leaving behind a trail of death and devastation. Southern towns such as Breda, were taken and recaptured many times. In 1574 the Dutch were forced to breach the dykes around Leiden to relieve the besieged city.

Initially the whole of the Low Countries had risen up in revolt. The nobility and the towns were aggrieved by Philip II's neglect of their privileges and independence, while the growing number of Protestants were alarmed by the increased powers of the Inquisition. But only the seven United Provinces of the north gained their independence.

The house of Orange

The Dutch were helped by the longer Spanish lines of communication, and the barrier of the great rivers often served to protect them. But their victory also came about as a result of the indomitable spirit of the people: their ruthless Sea Beggars, or commandos, who established the first Orange bridgehead at Brielle in 1572; their brave admirals; and above all, the leadership of William of Orange.

Owing to a misrendering of the Latin, William has come down to history as the Silent instead of the Sly. He needed all his diplomatic skill to hold this group of diverse, and often disputatious, provinces together; but he succeeded in his self-appointed task of forming a new nation. He was succeeded by Prince Maurice, a brilliant general, who helped to consolidate his father's success.

▼ In the more gracious days of the seventeenth century, musketeers were taught to raise their hats before they fired to kill. An engraving by Jacob de Gheyn from his *Waffenhandlung*, 1608, the first musketry drill book.

▼ *The Docker* was unveiled in an Amsterdam square in 1952. It commemorates the strike of Dutch workers in February 1941 against the Nazi anti-Jewish measures.

▼ The Dutch attack on the Medway, 1667, by Jan Peeters; a high point of one of three great naval wars with Britain. The Dutch were the last nation to invade England. Their gunfire could be heard in London.

▲ On January 21, 1795, the armies of revolutionary France crossed the frozen rivers and invaded the Netherlands. The Dutch republic, on its last legs, put up little resistance.

◄ The tradition of resistance was continued during the Second World War, when many Dutch risked their lives to copy BBC bulletins for the 1,200 underground papers.

▼ The Kabouters (gnomes) represent the modern spirit of independence. They want an alternative society based on peace, natural foods and help for the homeless. In 1970, 5 became Amsterdam councillors.

A passion for peace

▶ This statue, *Monument for a Devastated City*, symbolises the phoenix-like re-emergence of Rotterdam from the ashes of wartime devastation. The city was heavily bombed by the Germans in May, 1940.

A tradition of tolerance

For many centuries, Dutch society has been one of the most peaceful, humane and tolerant in the world. There has been very little persecution of people with minority views. Even during the Eighty Years' War with Catholic Spain, the city fathers of Amsterdam turned a blind eye towards the many Catholics who went on worshipping in their own way in the privacy of their homes. The burning of witches was stopped a century earlier than elsewhere. The Netherlands was the first country to grant full freedom to black slaves who were brought home by their masters, and one of the first to abolish capital punishment.

Throughout history, refugees have found a new home in the Netherlands. During the Eighty Years' War, thousands fled from the Spanish-held cities in the south to seek freedom and prosperity in the Dutch towns. Sephardim Jews from Spain and Portugal, and Ashkenazim from Poland and Germany

◀ One of the rare lapses from toleration occurred in 1619 when Grotius, the founder of international law, was imprisoned in Loevestein Castle. Two years later he escaped in a trunk, with the help of his wife.

A refuge for scholars

Towards the end of the seventeenth century a new wave of Huguenot refugees came in from France. Famous foreign scholars chose to live in this small country with its unusually great freedom to print controversial views. They included the philosophers John Locke, Rene Descartes and Baruch Spinoza.

The traditional qualities of humanity and tolerance, derived from Erasmus, have been preserved. Before World War II, many refugees from Nazi persecution were given asylum. But during the war, the Jewish population suffered greatly. Their hopes and fears are faithfully recorded in Anne Frank's diary, written while she was hiding in an Amsterdam house for two years. In recent times, Amsterdam has become an international refuge for hippies.

were given asylum and allowed to worship openly in their synagogues.

▲ In 1620, the Pilgrim Fathers left Delfshaven, Rotterdam, for the New World, via Plymouth. This band of English Puritans had been granted asylum first in Amsterdam, later in Leiden.

▲ The interior of the Peace Palace at The Hague. Built in 1913 with a grant from the American, Andrew Carnegie, it is the seat of the International Court of Justice.

▲ Delfshaven today. The old houses with their feet in the water, and the original Pilgrim's Church, are reminders of the past.

◀ Students from many developing countries come to take courses at The Hague. The building, a former palace, was given by the Queen to a Dutch foundation for international co-operation in 1952.

Patron of the arts

A nation on canvas

Dutch genius has always been mainly expressed in painting and drawing. In the seventeenth century, rich merchants bought and sold contemporary paintings on a big scale, encouraging the rise of the unique school of Dutch art. Their artists were masters of portraits, landscapes, still-lifes and realistic portrayals of everyday life. They were innovators of the new fashion for interior scenes, in which every detail of tiled floor, washbasin and cupboard was rendered with startling clarity. The history of European painting in that century is virtually a catalogue of Dutch names—

Rembrandt, Hals, Vermeer, de Hooch, Cuyp. Then artistic tradition slumbered, but it was revived in modern times by Van Gogh and Mondriaan. Today few countries are as blessed with such fine museums and galleries as the Netherlands. Artists are encouraged by the government and local authorities, and their works placed in hospitals and public buildings.

The other arts

The Dutch have also made some notable contributions in music, architecture and literature. Over 400 years ago, Adriaan Willaert put a choir on each side of a church to produce a stereophonic effect. Joost van den Vondel is rated as a major poet by the Dutch, though difficulties in translation have prevented much appreciation of his work elsewhere. Recently, painters, singers and ballet companies have made an international mark.

▼ *A Woman and Maid in a Courtyard* by Pieter de Hooch. Vermeer was another master of *genre* paintings, which show scenes from daily life.

▶ A detail from one of the many self-portraits by Rembrandt, the immortal genius of Dutch art. This painting is in Kenwood House, London.

▲ The artistic tradition is maintained by young and old, in city streets and in the countryside. Museums have special paint/study rooms.

▲ *Day and Night*, 1938, a woodcut by M.C. Escher. His works, masterpieces of illusion based on higher mathematics, are becoming increasingly popular.

▼ The sixteenth-century Gothic town hall in the marketplace at Middelburg is one of the finest in the country. It is decorated with statues of 25 counts and countesses.

▲ Jan van Huysum (1682-1749) was the greatest of Dutch flower painters. Superb detail and clarity of colour made him king in this most characteristic Dutch art form.

Merchants and seamen

▶ Tulips changed hands for thousands of guilders in the tulipomania of 1634-7. Many merchants were bankrupted when the speculative market crashed.

Cargo kings

The Dutch have long been the traders and carriers of Europe. Early in their history, a scarcity of natural resources forced many of them to seek their living on the sea. In the Middle Ages, Dutch herring busses, or boats, became the unrivalled masters of the fishing grounds in the North Sea.

Baltic trade was the 'mother' of Dutch prosperity but, in search of even greater profits, their ships started to sail into other seas. Towards the end of the sixteenth century they brought back the first Dutch cargoes of ivory and gold from West Africa and of spices from Java. The East India Company, founded in 1602, made handsome profits by dealing in exotic goods and laid the foundations for the empire overseas.

Sailors and salesmen

In the seventeenth century Amsterdam was the biggest *entrepôt* port—or centre for reception and distribution of goods—in the world. Its seamen were renowned for their skill, bravery and daring, while its huge fleets were the envy of foreign kings and statesmen. The *fluyt*, a freighter which was cheap to build and easy to sail, was bought by many other nations. Lucas van Waghenaer's marine charts were so accurate that they were used by many foreign seamen.

Now, as a founder member of the E.E.C., the Dutch are again at the forefront of trade. Rotterdam handles more tonnage than any other port in the world.

▲ Maarten Harpertszoon Tromp (1597-1653), depicted here as Neptune, was one of the greatest Dutch admirals. He went to sea at the age of eight and was credited with 30 victories over the Spanish and English.

▶ Dutch skills in seamanship helped to bring them victory in the Eighty Years' War. The Sea Beggars—a force of commandos—gained the first Orange foothold by capturing Brielle in 1572.

Am ersten des Monats Aprill, Verlor Duc D'Alba seinen brill.
Daß kan im sin gesicht gestochen, Vnd gelost schon vill stolzze knobe.

▼ A container lorry boarding the cross-Channel ferry, Queen Juliana, at the Hook of Holland. Dutch lorries—and barges—handle a large part of the internal transport of the EEC.

Colonies and exploration

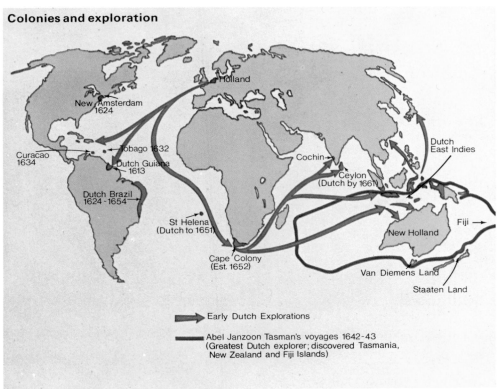

Holland

New Amsterdam 1624

Curacao 1634

Tobago 1632

Dutch Guiana 1613

Dutch Brazil 1624-1654

St Helena (Dutch to 1651)

Cape Colony (Est. 1652)

Cochin

Ceylon (Dutch by 1661)

Dutch East Indies

Fiji

New Holland

Van Diemens Land

Staaten Land

➤ Early Dutch Explorations

— Abel Janzoon Tasman's voyages 1642-43 (Greatest Dutch explorer; discovered Tasmania, New Zealand and Fiji Islands)

▲ In the seventeenth century Dutch seamen sailed the world in search of profit. But some discoveries, like Australia and New Zealand, were left to the British to exploit.

▼ Rotterdam-Europoort handles more goods than any other port in the world. It is the hub of sea-borne trade for the European Economic Community.

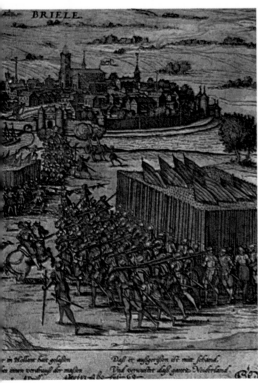

BRIELE

Sports and sportsmen

A nation of boundless energy

Sport is extremely popular in the Netherlands. About twenty per cent of the total population take part in some form of organised sport. To cater for their widely-differing interests, there are forty separate national organisations, which are subsidised by the government and by the football pools. The biggest organisation is the Royal Netherlands Football Association which has over 600,000 members.

Soccer is also the most popular spectator sport. When important matches are being shown on television, the streets and roads become almost totally deserted. Although professional football has been played only since the end of the war, Dutch teams have become a force to be reckoned with. Feyenoord of Rotterdam won the European Cup in 1970 and Ajax of Amsterdam were the winners in 1971 and 1972. Two years later the Netherlands was narrowly beaten by West Germany in the final of the World Cup.

Walking, cycling and skating

In summer, thousands of people, both young and old, take part in the four-day walking events which are held in various parts of the country. Yachting and cycling races are also very popular. Winter, if it's hard enough, makes practically the whole population take to the ice. Long-distance tours between towns are held on the frozen canals and lakes. Hastily-erected tents sell Dutch gin, fritters and pea soup to sustain the participants. On the IJsselmeer, sailing boats equipped with runners sweep across the ice at fantastic speeds.

In the post-war years Dutch men and women have carried off some major international prizes. The first woman to hit the world headlines was Fanny Blankers-Koen. Known as the Flying Housewife, she won three golds for sprinting and hurdling in the 1948 Olympics in London and helped to win another for the Dutch relay team. Ard Schenk has been world speed skating champion four times. Wim Ruska, the massive ex-sailor, won two gold medals for judo in the 1972 Olympic Games in Munich. And, of course, there is also Johan Cruyff, engaging champion of international soccer.

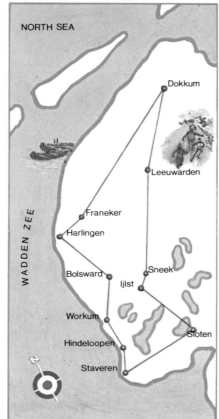

The Eleven Towns Race

NORTH SEA

WADDEN ZEE

Dokkum

Leeuwarden

Franeker

Harlingen

Bolsward

Sneek

Ijlst

Workum

Sloten

Hindeloopen

Staveren

The race covers about 150 miles. It starts and finishes in the provincial capital of Leeuwarden. Five thousand or more skaters start but only a few hundred finish the course. Because of weather conditions the race has been held only 12 times since 1909.

▲ The 11 Towns Race in Friesland over frozen lakes and canals—one of the most gruelling contests in the world.

▼ Johan Cruyff, super-star, in action in a World Cup match in 1974. A former Ajax player, he now plays for Barcelona.

▼ On canals, rivers, lakes and at sea, Dutch anglers spend many happy, but sometimes frustrating, hours. Inland fishermen have to possess a State licence.

► The Dutch share a passion for cycling with neighbouring Belgium. Four-day cycle rides are held in Almelo and Drenthe every July. Competitors begin young.

▼ Numerous lakes and the long coast line make the Netherlands a paradise for yacht-men. Yachting is one of the most popular sports.

Shops and shopping

Clever bargainers

When it comes to shopping the Dutch are both thrifty and cautious. There is very little impulse buying. Purchases are carefully calculated, sometimes many weeks ahead. The Dutch like to get a good bargain and they are willing to spend a long time making sure that they do.

Department stores, a feature of all large cities, offer a full range of international goods. Supermarkets have taken over much of the small shopkeeper's trade. But with their general desire to preserve the best features of the past, the Dutch have retained some of the old shopping traditions in the modern concrete setting.

Some supermarkets have a notice board where customers can display their 'wanted' and 'for sale' advertisements. The rather bleak alleys of some blocks of flats are made bright and bustling by the addition of old-time market stalls.

Souvenir of Holland

In the bigger cities, particularly Amsterdam, The Hague, Delft and Breda, there are many antique shops. Much of this trade is international, which is reflected in the prices. For those with less money to spend, there are souvenir shops selling costumed dolls in protective plastic cases, clogs or wooden shoes, and blue-and-white glazed tiles or pottery. Genuine Delft pottery, which is also red, white and polychrome, is now made only in two factories. It remains a favourite take-home present for tourists.

Service in souvenir shops is sometimes surprisingly thoughtful. It is not unknown for even a small, cheap gift to be wrapped in a gay gift paper and ornately tied with a coloured ribbon free of charge. Many shopkeepers speak English, as the learning of two foreign languages is a compulsory part of the four-year-course at retail trade schools.

Shops generally open on weekdays between 8.30 and 9 a.m. and close either at 5.30 or 6 p.m. Some of them close for lunch between 1 and 2 p.m. Many department stores are closed on Monday mornings.

▲ The guilder, or florin, is divided into 100 cents. There are 5, 10, 25, 100 and 1,000 guilder notes. The coins are 1, 5, 10, 25 cents; the guilder; and the *rijksdaalder*, f2.50.

◄ Clogs come in handy on the open decks of barges which make up Singel flower market in Amsterdam. In spring and summer it makes the city centre blaze with colour.

► The colourful clog market at Alkmaar, North Holland, attracts an interested crowd. Few Dutch people wear wooden shoes, but they have a lively sale among foreign tourists.

▼ Dried fish, shellfish and white fish are all to be found on market stalls, where women still cry their wares as they have done for centuries.

► Flea markets are popular with foreigners and the Dutch, who are always looking for a bargain. Some hidden treasures may be found among the plastic bowls, kettles, books and bric-a-brac.

▼ Shopping is easy in the car-free streets which are found in most big cities, though pedestrians still have to watch out for trams and the odd cyclist.

Eating the Dutch way

▶ A full-size *rijsttafel* (literally rice-table) consists of twenty or so separate dishes. These include rice; curried and steamed meat, meat in Java sauce, and roast pork; tomatoes, cucumbers and fruit in various sauces; fried mushrooms, bananas and coconut; vegetables in a peanut sauce, bean sprouts and spices. The meat is usually moistened with a thin, tasty, vegetable soup. Dutch lager is usually drunk with this gargantuan meal for gourmets, or sometimes a dry rosé or white wine. The Dutch also like other Indonesian dishes, such as *bami goreng* or *nasi goreng*—noodles or rice with meat and vegetables.

Dutch treats

Dutch food is plain and simple. Their soups, which are usually home-made, are excellent. Vegetables are also of high quality, particularly asparagus, carrots, tomatoes and cabbage. In the seventeenth century, the Dutch were known throughout Europe as 'butter mouths', but most of them, even the wealthy, now eat margarine. It was first produced on a commercial scale in the Netherlands in the 1870s.

One of the great gastronomic feasts—the celebrated Zeeland oyster—is fast disappearing. The Delta project, a flood prevention scheme, has spelt the oysters' doom, as their breeding grounds will be transformed into freshwater lakes.

Some of the best food in the whole country has its origins in the former colony of Indonesia. Almost every town has a variety of restaurants serving this delicious spicy food. The classic speciality is *rijsttafel*.

Dutch specialities

Pea Soup

Put 1 lb. dried split peas, 2 pig's feet, 8 oz. salt pork and 6½ pts. water into large casserole. Bring to boil, simmer for 3 hrs. Add 4 potatoes in ¼ in. dice, 4 finely chopped leeks, 1 med. cereriac (or celery) peeled and diced, and 3 celery leaves. Cook 30 min. Remove salt pork and pig's feet; trim, clean and dice meat, return to soup with 8 oz. sliced kielbasa, ¼ tsp. summer savory and pepper. Heat and serve.

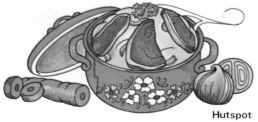

Erwtensoep

Hot Pot

Bring 1½ pts. water to boil in heavy casserole. Add 1½ tea. salt and 2 lb. fresh brisket of beef. Bring back to boil, partially cover and reduce heat. Simmer for 2½-3 hrs. Add 2 lb. diced carrots, cook 30 min. longer. Add 3 lb. potatoes, and 10 coarsely chopped onions. Simmer until liquid mostly evaporated. Mash vegetables, place meat on top and serve with sharp mustard and pickles.

Hutspot

Apple Fritters

Sift 8 oz. flour into a mixing bowl. Pour ¾ pt. beer into flour; mix till smooth. Set aside for 3 hours. 15 minutes before making fritters, peel and core 5 apples, cut into ⅓ in. thick rounds. Mix 8 oz. sugar, 2½ tsp. cinnamon, together; sprinkle rounds on both sides. Pour vegetable oil into deep-fryer to depth of 3 in. and heat to 375°. Dip each apple slice into batter, fry for 3-4 min. Keep warm till serving.

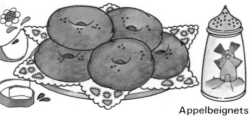

Appelbeignets

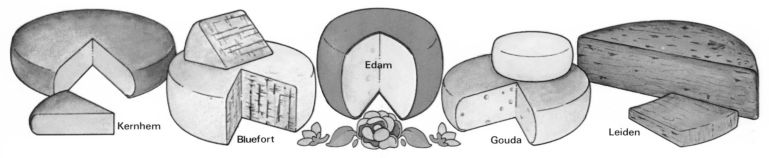

Kernhem   Bluefort   Edam   Gouda   Leiden

► A typical day's menu for a Dutch family.
1. Breakfast: usually coffee or cocoa with various kinds of bread, with a spread of cheese and ham; more often than not, margarine is preferred to butter. 2. Elevenses: sweet pastry and coffee or tea. 3. Lunch: hot soup, salad and a selection of sandwiches, including the famous *uitsmijter* or egg-topped open-face. 4. Tea: tea or coffee and "cookies" — the original Dutch sweet biscuit. 5. Dinner: soup, pot roast and vegetable, followed by a plum tart.

◄ Dutch gin, or *jenever*, is a very popular drink. It's a great challenge to drain it without touching the glass.

▼ The Dutch have their own unique titbits: slivers of raw, salted herring and smoked eel.

A typical day's menu

► Clean sandwich shops (*broodjeswinkels*), with refrigerated cabinets, serve cheap snacks and hot soups.

▼ Pancakes, savoury or sweet, are a traditional treat; no holds are barred.

Amsterdam—Venice of the North

A city built on water

Amsterdam, the capital of the Netherlands, is one of the most fascinating and attractive cities in Europe. From small beginnings in the Middle Ages, when two men and a dog settled on the bank of the river Amstel, it grew into a fishing and trading port. Its official birth came in 1275 when the powerful Count of Holland freed the people living around the dam in the Amstel from paying tolls.

The dam has disappeared, but its existence is still commemorated in the name of the main square. No other city, not even Venice, owes so much to the arduous toil of its own citizens. Over the centuries the size of this low-lying city has been continually increased by draining more land. There was a great expansion in the seventeenth century when three new major canals were constructed—the Herengracht, the Keizersgracht and the Prinsengracht. Long, wooden piles were sunk through the sandy, waterlogged soil to firmer strata, to provide foundations for handsome merchant's houses. That masterpiece of Dutch Renaissance architecture, the Royal Palace in Dam Square, rests on 13,659 piles.

Amsterdam remains a beautifully preserved slice of seventeenth century history. It is divided by its concentric ring of canals into ninety islands connected by over six hundred bridges. On some quiet nights when the water is lapping against the banks of the canal and the wind is rustling the leaves of the bordering lime trees, it is still possible to imagine that some breeched and ruffed merchant may emerge from his house onto the uneven pavement.

Modern metropolis

But Amsterdam is not all history. It is still a thriving, modern port and the centre of the biggest industrial complex in the country, with a large stake in the shipbuilding, metal, brewing, car and aircraft industries. One of the newest developments is the huge off-the-peg clothing centre near Schiphol airport. It is also the printing, publishing, financial and banking centre.

▼ The heart of the capital is Dam Square, with its gleaming white monument to Dutch victims of the Second World War. In the background there is the Royal Palace, built in the seventeenth century as a town hall.

▲ Amsterdam abounds in old merchant houses, with stepped gables and projecting hooks for hauling goods up to the top floors.

► Kalverstraat, the international shopping street, with its own Madame Tussaud's.

KEY
1 Amstelkring Museum
2 Old Church
3 Royal Palace
4 Zoo and Aquarium
5 Rembrandt's House
6 University
7 Rijksmuseum

Amsterdam—a masterpiece of design

▲ Only a few steps from Kalverstraat, but centuries away in time. Begijnhof is a dignified square with almshouses and the English Church.

▼ Tree-lined canals, barges and ancient monuments, like the Mint Tower, 1620, give the capital its unique appeal.

Monarchy and the Hague

Status and statesmen

The Hague, which is the seat of government and the diplomatic centre, is the most elegant—and the most status-conscious—town in the country. It is a city of broad boulevards, landscaped gardens and shady woods, tree-lined canals and flower-filled shopping arcades. The most spectacular building is the thirteenth-century Hall of Knights in the *Binnenhof*, where Parliament meets. Majestic swans glide on the adjoining ornamental lake.

Ever since Count William II of Holland started to build a hunting lodge in the *Binnenhof* in 1247, the Hague has had close connections with the country's leading family. During the republic, the stadholders had their court in the Hague. Even though the Queen now lives some miles away in the village of Soestdijk, and monarchs, by tradition, are inaugurated in the capital of Amsterdam, it is still the official royal residence.

A democratic queen

The Dutch monarchy is very democratic. Although William II had a crown made in 1840, it is rarely worn but only displayed. Queen Juliana has ridden a bicycle in the streets and her daughters went to the local primary school.

▲ The Royal Standard. The lion, derived from the crest of William of Orange, symbolizes authority and might.

▲ Statues of judges adorn the façade of the Supreme Court of Justice in the Hague.

◀ Parks and fields are not far away from the city centre with its lake and thirteenth century Hall of Knights in the Binnenhof, centre.

▲ The Royal Family. Queen Juliana sits centre, with Prince Bernhard behind her. Princess Beatrix is on her right.

▶ Liveried footmen accompany the golden coach as the queen arrives to open parliament on the third Tuesday in September.

▲ Floodlights and reflections in the still waters of Vijver lake bring a touch of majesty to government buildings.

◀ Prime Minister, J. M. den Uyl, addressing the Lower House of Parliament in The Hague. Statements are usually read.

Farms and factories

Green fields

Dairy farming, horticulture and food-processing are still mainstays of the economy as they have been for many years. The lush green pastures of the reclaimed polders are ideally suited to grazing cattle. Milk from the high-yielding Friesian cows is made into butter, cheese or condensed milk in modern factories, which are often run as co-operatives. Hundreds of acres of glass give horticulturists an edge over their northern competitors in getting early vegetables and flowers on to the international market first.

But the quick pace of industry is over-taking the steady grind of agriculture. The Dutch were slow to take part in the first industrial revolution. Railways and factories with steam-powered engines were built much later than in many European countries. The first big steel plant was not

◀ Paint shop of the Daf car plant, Eindhoven. A Dutch product recently acquired by Volvo, a Swedish firm, the cars are renowned for their automatic transmission.

▼ Friesians, the chief breed of cattle in Holland, are now popular in many countries.

opened until the First World War when supplies from Germany were reduced.

And new horizons

The Dutch have been much quicker to participate in the second industrial revolution based on oil, natural gas, chemicals and electronics. They have been helped by the early development of multi-national companies such as Philips, Royal Dutch/Shell and Unilever; the discovery of huge natural gas fields in Groningen; and the growth of Rotterdam as an industrial port following the formation of the E.E.C.

At the same time there has been a rapid expansion of industry, particularly in the metallurgical and petro-chemical sectors. Industry employs about 40 per cent of the working population. The real national income doubled in the 1958-1971 period.

Diamond centre of the world

▲ Amsterdam is the heart of the diamond industry. The gems are first sawn into two by a revolving blade.

▲ The stone is then polished to give it the usual 58 sparkling facets, which makes it every girl's best friend.

▼ The wholesale flower market at Aalsmeer, North Holland. In Dutch auctions prices start high. The first bidder becomes the buyer, hence the phrase "Dutch auction"

▲ The rough stones are cut into the required shape. This can only be done against another diamond.

▲ Rotterdam-Europoort has become one of the biggest oil refineries and chemical complexes in western Europe.

▼ Age-old tradition makes the cheese market at Alkmaar, North Holland, a combined tourist and trading success. There is a similar market at Gouda, South Holland.

▲ Diamonds come in different shapes and sizes. Their value is judged by their colour, clarity, cut and weight.

Time off

For the visitor

The Netherlands offers a great diversity of attractions for foreign tourists. People come from all parts of the world to see the brilliant splashes of colour in the tulip fields between Haarlem and Leiden in the spring. The Keukenhof open-air show of flowering bulbs at Lisse, South Holland, provides an equally great attraction at the same time.

The bicycle, that typical Dutch mode of transport, is one of the best ways to see the country. A fine system of cycle paths, and the number of inexpensive hostels and pensions which cater to the two-wheeled traveller, make legwork the only effort.

Amsterdam, with its swinging night life, is the third or fourth most popular tourist capital in Europe. There are many sights worth seeing both in the city and outside. One of the most popular is the small town of Marken where regional costumes are still worn as part of daily life. The Holland Festival of concerts and exhibitions, held at the end of June and the beginning of July, has started to attract an increasing number of discerning patrons of the arts.

And the Dutch

Many of the Dutch go to different parts of the country for their holidays. Friesland, with its numerous lakes, canals and sandy beaches is a paradise for sailors, anglers, or those who just like a quiet life. The large number of nature reserves contain some of the most important sanctuaries for water birds and waders in Europe.

All along the North Sea coast there is mile after mile of unspoilt, but windswept, beaches. Walking across the sand dunes can be relaxing, but it is not always free. A charge is made in some areas. Scheveningen, near the Hague, is the most popular seaside resort. But many of the Dutch now drive off in the family car to Spain or Italy in search of the sun.

▲ Dress (almost) as you please! Wicker chairs offer their protection from the wind to all ages at Zandvoort, a popular holiday resort near Haarlem.

▲ A common form of winter entertainment, when the ice holds, is skating on the frozen lakes and canals. The popular conception of Holland as the land of the skate has survived recent mild winters.

◄ Mud-walking in Friesland. One of the strangest recreations in Europe is walking across the Wadden Sea to the offshore islands at low tide. Take a Dutchman with you!

▲ Human beings become Gullivers in this scale model of a typical Dutch town at Madurodam, The Hague. Everything works. Trains run; cars move; the band plays.

◄ Music is popular with the Dutch. The Amsterdam Concertgebouw Orchestra has achieved world-wide renown.

▲ Not everything is flat. Valkenburg, and other places in Limburg, have hills and old castles, perfect for picnics and hiking.

Waterways and bicycles

▲ One of the most unusual roads in Europe, between the North Sea and Lake IJssel. It runs along the top of the retaining dam.

▲ Dutch barges lined up, a dozen or more abreast, in Rotterdam harbour. About 40 per cent of their work consists of carrying goods along canals and rivers to ports in other EEC countries.

▶ The Dutch started the first scheduled internal transport system in the seventeenth century. Canal barges, *trekschuiten,* carried passengers and goods from town to town. They left at the ringing of a bell.

The land of the bicycle

Getting about is no problem in the Netherlands as the country is not only small but also mainly flat. As a result, bicycles have retained their popularity with men and women, young and old, the rich and the not-so-rich. Everyone rides a bike, from the royals down. Tiresome traffic jams easily build up in the narrow streets by the canals or on the small hump-backed bridges. While the car driver fumes, the cyclist pedals past.

No other people can ride a bicycle with such self-assurance as the Dutch. They cycle through a fearsome stream of moving cars and lorries as if they were having a quiet ride in a park. Although the odds are stacked against them, they insist on claiming their legal priority when they are going straight on at a road junction. The motorist who wants to turn right, across their path, is warned to beware.

In all there are about seven million bicycles and another two million *brommers* or mopeds. Bikes can be bought new or secondhand or hired. Auctions are held in Amsterdam every fortnight or so.

Trains, boats and planes

But it is not all bikes. The Netherlands has one of the finest communication networks in the whole of Europe. There are good straight motorways, an efficient train service, and the nation's pride, KLM, the oldest established airline in the world.

▲ Bicycles, of all shapes and sizes, are parked in concrete racks. Trams also provide quick and efficient transport in many of the big cities.

▲ The only way to get about in Giethoorn is by boat along the waterways, or along the rough track by the canals. There are no streets in the village.

▶ Schiphol airport, near Amsterdam, with its four runways, is the biggest in the country and the headquarters of KLM.

Media and communication

An airing to all views

Very few organisations have a simple structure in the Netherlands, and TV is no exception. In the early days of radio in the 1920s, five associations—political, religious and 'neutral'—gained a monopoly of air time by paying for the programmes and the necessary equipment. When television transmissions started in 1951, they continued to provide the majority of programmes. The government, however, set up another body to provide studies, technical facilities and some programmes, such as the news.

This system, which built *verzuiling* into the mass media, did not please everybody. The Dutch have been trying to break it down ever since, with pirate TV transmissions from the North Sea and political pressure. The issue aroused so much passion that it caused the downfall of the government in 1965.

Variety—spice or starch?

Since then the studio doors have been thrown open to a variety of newcomers. The former 'pirates' have joined the five established associations. Smaller political and religious groups have been granted limited air time. Other bodies concerned with social problems, such as drugs and child welfare, have been given a chance to broadcast as part of an on-going programme of social reform. At the same time, revenue has been increased by allowing a limited number of advertisements, mainly before and after the news.

In theory, such an open system might be expected to produce some lively television. In practice, however, programmes are often rather didactic and dull. But the Dutch have their escape routes. Their facility in languages and the proximity of Germany and of Belgium allow them to turn over to other channels. Many of them do so.

▲ The Dutch have always been internationally minded. Dutch, French and English mingle happily in the posters on this advertising kiosk. About 65 per cent of the Dutch can speak English, many of them extremely well. They usually speak another language, too.

▲ The multilingual Dutch read many foreign magazines as well as those produced in their own language. Newspapers are usually delivered on subscription to the door.

▼ A television studio in the radio-TV city of Hilversum. The studios and the equipment are provided for the use of TV companies by a State organisation, the NOS.

▼ The Dutch produced the first newspapers in Europe. This rare copy was printed in Amsterdam by Joris Veseler in 1618. It gave reports of wars and royal scandals from foreign parts. Some papers were printed in the English language.

Courante uyt Italien, Duytslandt, &c.

[Early 17th-century Dutch newspaper text, printed in blackletter, 1618]

▲ Missing the post Dutch-style. Until recently trams carried letters to the central sorting office in Amsterdam. "Slipping" a letter into the box could mean just that !

▼ Television companies rely heavily on programmes imported from other countries. Commercials are shown before and after the news.

▲ Take your medicine like a *gaper* ! At one time chemists used the tongues of these little effigies to display their pills.

A typical day on TV
Channel 1
18.25 *Tour de France:* cycle race
18.45 Little Windmills: children's programme
18.55 News
19.05 National hit parade: pop music
20.21 Who knows ?: prize quiz show
21.40 I sing of Amsterdam: musical celebration of city's seven hundredth anniversary
22.30 *Televizier* Magazine: current affairs
23.15 Along Christ's Way: interview with missionary
Channel 2
18.55 News
19.05 The Roadmakers on Sea show: cabaret series
19.30 Cock of the Roost: quiz show on TV programmes
20.00 Main news and weather outlook
20.20 Top or Flop ?: pop records
20.50 Hallo, here is Hilversum: variety show
22.00 Portrait: documentary about handicapped youth
22.30 The Chief Inspector: German crime series
23.30 Interview with Prime Minister: weekly series
23.40 Late News

Customs and costumes

▶ Birthdays of the extended family are carefully noted on a calendar. It is usually hung on the back of the kitchen or lavatory door.

▼ Traditional costumes are not tourist baits but part of the way of life in Volendam, north of Amsterdam. They are also worn in some other small villages.

Family and faith

Not unnaturally, the family is the focus of many public and private celebrations in the Netherlands. Birthdays are observed as they are nowhere else, with gifts, parties and congratulations for all. The Queen's birthday, on April 30, transforms the whole nation into one big family, with loyal citizens presenting gifts in person to the monarch at Soestdijk palace.

The birthday of St. Nicholas, the patron saint of children, is also another big occasion. Colourful processions are watched by thousands of spectators. The saint rides his white horse attended by Black Piet, his servant. Children now expect to receive presents both at Christmas and on his birthday, December 6.

Superstitions still prevail in isolated villages. Some small farmers in Zeeland refused to help with rescue operations during the 1953 floods which, they believed, were the will of God. In 1971, some Staphorst villagers refused to have vaccine in a polio epidemic.

▼ Clogs were once worn in most parts of the country, but they have become an increasingly rare sight — except in souvenir shops. There are six main stages in making them.

1. The block of wood is cut with an axe.

2. It is trimmed into shape with a matchet . . .

4. The interior is gouged out . . .

5. and it is smoothed with a rod.

Regional attitudes

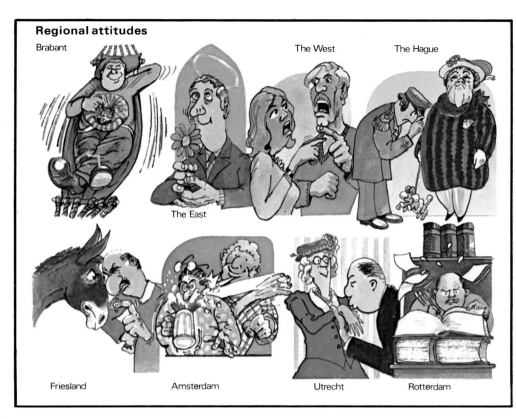

Brabant

The West

The Hague

The East

Friesland

Amsterdam

Utrecht

Rotterdam

◀ How the Dutch traditionally see themselves. The people of the West are good-natured; those of the East more argumentative. The Brabanters love an easy life; people from The Hague are considered snobbish. The Frisians are stubborn; the Amsterdammer slap-happy and jolly. The citizens of Utrecht have gentle, old-fashioned manners, while Rotterdammers plough into work!

▶ The Dutch love collecting small objects. and souvenirs. The habit started in the seventeenth century when sailors brought back shells and other mementoes from overseas.

▼ Colourful barrel organs still bring their tinkling tunes to city streets. Carillons add their notes from towers.

3. to give the rough form of a wooden shoe.

6. Finally, the clog is gaily painted.

Heroes in fact and fiction

Men of skill and courage

With their down-to-earth attitudes, the Dutch have never gone in for much hero-worship. They expect people to live up to their positions and they are more likely to condemn those who fail, than to praise those who succeed. They reserve most of their adulation for the men who helped to form the nation and for those who still help to maintain it.

Michael de Ruyter, their greatest admiral, now receives much more veneration than he did in the seventeenth century. Sir William Temple, the English ambassador, was astonished to find that he walked about the streets unattended—like a common sea captain.

Piet Heyn is another admiral who is still remembered for his great feat of capturing the Spanish silver fleet off Cuba in 1628. In a typical anti-hero way, Heyn himself complained that his other victories at sea had been greater and more difficult, but ignored.

Women of conviction

In modern times, the Dutch have made their queens their heroines. During the German occupation in the last war, Queen Wilhelmina's broadcasts from exile in London kept up the spirit of resistance in her people. They expressed their gratitude at her death in 1962: the only wreath on her bier was one from war-time resistance groups.

A great storm blew up in 1966 when Princess Beatrix's marriage to a German revived bitter memories of the occupation. The storm has passed. Prince Claus is now as widely accepted as the consort, Prince Bernhard, who is also of German blood!

▼ Almost everyone has heard the story of the Dutch boy with his finger in the dyke who saved his village from being flooded. Though the tale was invented by an American writer, Mary Mapes Dodge, a statue to "The hero of Haarlem" stands in Spaarndam.

▲ William of Orange, 'the Father of the Fatherland', is still venerated by the Dutch. During a time of religious warfare, he was an opportunist of the best sort. Tolerance and moderation were his constant plea. Born in 1533, Count of Nassau, he inherited the principality of Orange and large estates in the Low Countries. The House of Orange-Nassau has produced the country's stadholders and monarchs ever since.

▲ The legendary ship, *The Flying Dutchman*, with its ghostly captain and crew, is an omen of ill-luck, doomed to sail the seas for ever.

▲ Michael de Ruyter (1607-1676) retained the unpretentious manners of his humble upbringing in Zeeland. The men who sailed with him affectionately called him Grandad.

▼ St. Nicholas is the friendly hero of children not only in the Netherlands but also in many other countries. Santa Claus is a corrupt form form of the Dutch 'Santa Klaus'.

▲ The bronze statue to Desiderius Erasmus, the father of humanism, in his birthplace of Rotterdam. It was unveiled in April, 1622.

A sturdy independence

The public person

The Dutch character is highly deceptive. Some foreigners dismiss the Dutchman as dull, unimaginative, mean, earnest and respectable.

All of that is true in part. History has made these people thrifty, cautious and conventional. Merely to survive they have had to struggle hard—against the sea, against their powerful neighbours. Living by trade, they have had to be determined. The Dutch are still among the hardest bargainers on earth. Their very existence has been such a gamble that they do not like to take unnecessary risks. Their country is so overcrowded, and was once so divided against itself, that they have had to make many rules and learn to live with them.

And the private

But there is also another aspect. Inside the respectable Dutchman, there is often a fiercely independent and rebellious character struggling to get out. They have been forced to keep their feet firmly on their waterlogged ground, but their heads are frequently in the clouds. Causes can arouse the Dutchman's passion and break down their controls.

Do the Dutch have a sense of humour? Most foreigners—and many of the Dutch themselves—think that they do not. But others believe, rightly, that in a broader way, they do have a quiet sense of fun.

The Dutch have learnt to live with many different kinds of people, both at home and abroad. Through painful experience, they have learnt that accommodation pays. There are few other people who are so publicly tolerant of others, though in private it is often different. Their main virtues are their respect for the individual, their sense of social justice, and their delight in order.

▲ Be kind to your feathered friends! The road sign warns motorists—and the ubiquitous cyclist—to stop.

▼ The Dutch like to know what's going on around them. The *spionnetje*—spy mirror—on the outside wall helps them to find out.

▼ The Dutch have always been rather stiff and formal in their manners and dress. During the seventeenth century men and women started to abandon the starched ruff in favour of more flowing garments. But the tradition of respectability was retained. It helped to lay the foundations of a bourgeois society.

▼ Nothing is wasted in the Netherlands. Discarded petals from the tulip fields are used to make this float at Keukenhof.

▲ The Dutch don't buy many goods on hire purchase. It takes a lot of thought—and even more saving—to fill a bare room.

▲ Foreigners have always been amazed by the Dutch passion for cleanliness. The annual spring clean still dominates family life.

A progressive society

► 'Mad Minnies', named after the Dutch feminist Wilhelmina Drucker, lead the fight for equal rights.

A twenty-year renaissance

In the last two decades, the Netherlands has changed radically. Once among the most backward countries in north-west Europe, it is now one of the most progressive.

Twenty years ago the Roman Catholic church was doctrinaire and very conservative. Women had the vote, but lacked many other rights. They could not have a bank account of their own and were not allowed to marry without their parents' consent until they were thirty. The old Protestant establishment still had a dominating role in society and politics.

In 1954 the country started to transform itself as a result of a three-fold shock. The German invasion of 1940 destroyed the cozy myth of neutrality. The loss of Indonesia in 1949 deprived the country of an immense source of wealth. Finally, the 1953 floods brought the Dutch face to face with the basic insecurity of their own situation yet again.

The new Netherlands

Since then, the Netherlands has become a different country. The Catholic church is one of the most progressive in Europe. Rapid industrialisation has brought about a great increase in wealth. Women have gained much greater rights—though they still want more—and society has become increasingly open. The Provos and later the Kabouters (gnomes) were the first groups in Europe to attract widespread attention with their protests against pollution and their proposals for an alternative society.

▲ The mushroom-shaped Evoluon Exhibition at Eindhoven was built by Philips in 1966 to celebrate the firm's seventy-fifth anniversary. The company is eighth largest in the Common Market.

► White-faced clowns play folk and beat music on their guitars by the National Monument in Amsterdam. Until recently, Dam Square was an international rendezvous for dropouts every summer.

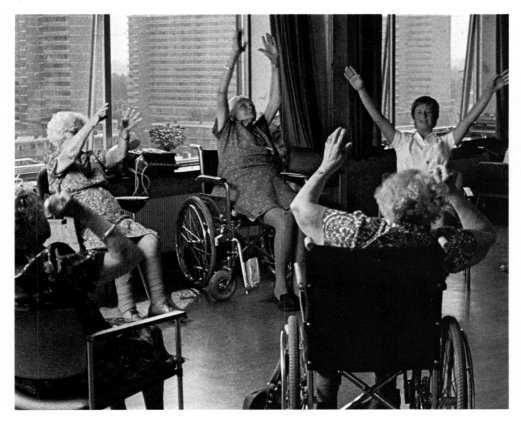

▲ Gymnastics from the wheelchair. Dutch concern for the handicapped is also shown in the model village of Het Dorp, Arnhem.

► The Dutch have always been leaders in the fight against the sea. The flood-prevention Delta scheme is due to be completed by 1978. The earlier Zuider Zee reclamation scheme is almost finished.

▼ Policemen—and soldiers—wear their hair long. The Dutch like to keep up with the times, though sometimes they are a little over-eager and go too far.

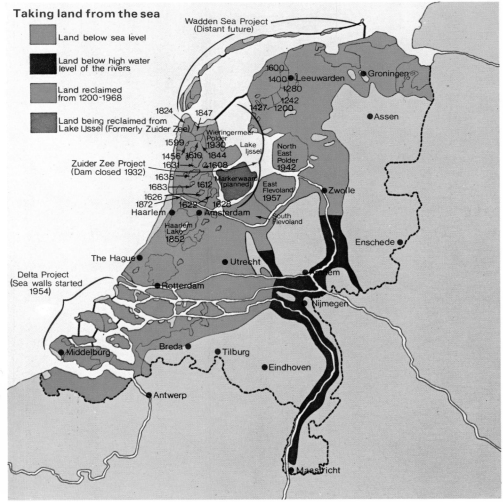

Taking land from the sea

- Land below sea level
- Land below high water level of the rivers
- Land reclaimed from 1200-1968
- Land being reclaimed from Lake IJssel (Formerly Zuider Zee)

Wadden Sea Project (Distant future)

Zuider Zee Project (Dam closed 1932)

Delta Project (Sea walls started 1954)

Wieringermeer Polder 1930

North East Polder 1942

East Flevoland 1957

South Flevoland

Markerwaard (planned)

Haarlem Lake 1852

Groningen
Leeuwarden
Assen
Lake IJssel
Zwolle
Enschede
Utrecht
Arnhem
Nijmegen
The Hague
Rotterdam
Haarlem
Amsterdam
Middelburg
Breda
Tilburg
Eindhoven
Antwerp
Maastricht

Reference
Human and physical geography

The Climate of the Netherlands

The Royal Netherlands Meteorological Institute is located at De Bilt, not far from Utrecht. As the climatic conditions throughout the country are so uniform, data provided from this centre serves the whole of the Netherlands. This information is relayed to farming areas, Schiphol airport, and other centres to whom weather is business.

The Netherlands has a marine climate, with generally mild winters and cool summers. It is practically uniform all over the country. The prevailing winds are westerly and south-westerly, with a late spring period of cool north-westerly winds. There can be severe frosts in the spring; heavy downfalls of rain in the summer; and strong winds, particularly along the coast and in the west, at almost any season. The mean winter temperature is around 2.6°C, while the mean summer temperature is about 18.1°C. Mean average rainfall per month varies between 5.6 cm. and 8.2 cm.; the wettest regions are the northeast, the Veluwe area and southern Limburg, with heaviest falls from July to September. Marsh mists and sea fog are common, particularly in winter. Although the sky often seems clouded, there are on average 1,500 hours of sunshine a year.

Natural vegetation

Forest Vegetation
Coniferous Forest & Shrub
Mixed Broad-leaved & Coniferous Woodland
Mixed Broad-leaved Woodland & Meadow

Grass Vegetation
Valley Grassland
Meadowland
Peat & Sandy Polderland
Shrub, Heath & Marshy Grassland

Desert Vegetation
Sandy Coastal Wastes

The population density

Inhabitants	
per mile²	per km²
under 128	under 50
128-256	50-100
256-512	100-200
over 512	over 200

Apart from some small states such as Macao, Monaco and Hong Kong, the Netherlands is the most densely populated country in the world with 390 people to the square kilometre. The population is unevenly distributed throughout the country. Nearly half of the total population (46.3 per cent) live in the *Randstad*, the horseshoe-shaped complex of towns and cities in the west, where the density rises to 900 per square kilometre.

Since the end of the Second World War, the Netherlands has experienced the biggest migratory movements in its history. About half a million Dutch men and women have emigrated, mainly to Canada, Australia and the United States. This has been partly balanced by the immigration of Dutch settlers and officials, Eurasians and natives from Indonesia, which was granted independence in 1949. This flow of immigrants had almost dried up, when new waves from Surinam began to arrive. Since 1961 there has usually been a net surplus of immigrants, mainly workers from other European countries.

Population of principal cities

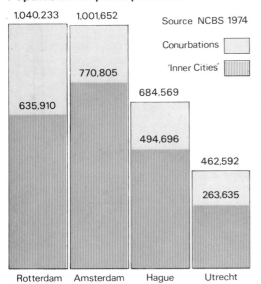

Source NCBS 1974

Conurbations
'Inner Cities'

Rotterdam	1,040,233 / 635,910
Amsterdam	1,001,652 / 770,805
Hague	684,569 / 494,696
Utrecht	462,592 / 263,635

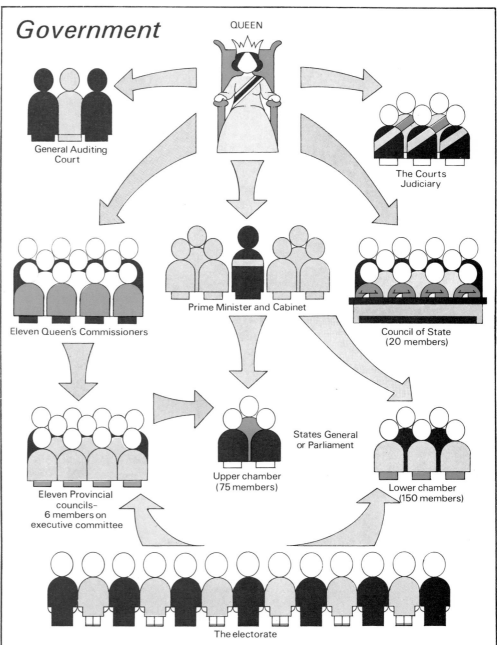

Government

QUEEN

General Auditing Court

The Courts Judiciary

Eleven Queen's Commissioners

Prime Minister and Cabinet

Council of State (20 members)

Eleven Provincial councils– 6 members on executive committee

States General or Parliament

Upper chamber (75 members)

Lower chamber (150 members)

The electorate

The Dutch system of government is based on compromise. Proportional representation ensures that many fringe parties have a voice in the States-General, or parliament, even though their influence may be small. As no one party ever gains an outright victory at the polls, governments are always coalitions of up to five larger parties. In the process of forming a coalition, party leaders are forced to make many concessions before a common policy can be formulated.

Parliament has the supreme power of voting out the government, but in practice it is rarely used. Both houses confine themselves mainly to stating their views, questioning ministers and instituting enquiries. Only the second chamber can amend bills or introduce legislation. The first chamber, which is elected indirectly by provincial councils, can only approve or reject bills. Ministers do not sit in parliament, though they appear in both houses regularly to explain their bills or to defend their views.

The Queen is no mere figurehead. She presides over the Council of State which advises on all bills. She also appoints the *formateur* who tries to get agreement among party leaders when a new coalition government is being formed.

The system produces relatively stable government. But critics complain that it gives too much power to party leaders and to the establishment, which makes many important decisions *in camera*.

Reference
History

Main events in Dutch history
B.C.

c. 4000	Central European tribes settle in Limburg.
c. 2700	Tribes from eastern Europe in Drenthe.
c. 2200	Invasion of Veluwe by tribes from east.
c. 800	Tribes from Switzerland and Rhineland settle south of great rivers.
c. 300	Frisians arrive in north.
57	Roman invasion of Rhine and Scheldt estuaries.

A.D.

12	Conquest by Romans under Nero Claudius Drusus.
28	Frisian revolt.
69	Batavian revolt led by Civilis.
250-75	Frankish invasions.
c. 400	Roman troops start to withdraw.
c. 450	Angles and Saxons invade Friesland.
c. 450-734	Frisians dominant in north; Saxons in east; Franks in south.
c. 690	St. Willibrord in Utrecht.
734	Franks defeat Frisians and drive them north of Rhine.
c. 840	Viking invasions start.
843	Frankish middle kingdom under Lothar 1.
855	Lothar dies; middle kingdom split up.
925	Eastern Franks rule Low Countries.
1000-1300	Feudal counts increase powers.
1384	Philip the Bold, Duke of Burgundy, extends dominions in Low Countries.
1464	Philip the Good, Duke of Burgundy, institutes States-General (Parliament).
1477	Mary, Duchess of Burgundy, marries Archduke Maximilian of the House of Habsburg.
1543	Habsburg Charles V unites the 17 provinces.
1550s	Calvinism gains adherents.
1555	Charles V abdicates; Philip II of Spain rules Low Countries.
1559	Philip leaves for Spain; half-sister, Margaret, Duchess of Parma, regent.
1566	Revolt in Low Countries against Inquisition.

The Eighty Years' War

1568	Duke of Alva crushes revolt.
1572	Sea Beggars capture Brielle.
1574	Siege of Leiden.
1575	Leiden University founded.
1579	Union of Utrecht between Holland, Zeeland, Utrecht and Gelderland; later also Friesland, Groningen and Overijssel.
1581	William of Orange (known as the Silent) and United Provinces renounce allegiance to Philip.
1584	William the Silent assassinated.
1585	Prince Maurice, William's son, appointed stadholder of Holland and Zeeland.
1590-4	Maurice regains Groningen, Overijssel and Breda.
1602	Dutch East Indies Company founded.
1605	Dutch capture Amboina.
1609	Twelve years' truce.
1618-9	Synod of Dort—disputes between Gomarists (strict Calvinists) and Arminians. Execution of the Arminian, Johan van Oldenbarneveldt, Advocate of Holland.
1621	Dutch West India Company.
1624	New Amsterdam founded on Manhattan Island.
1625	Frederick Henry succeeds Maurice.
1628	Piet Heyn captures Spanish silver fleet off Cuban coast.
1634-7	Tulipomania.
1637	Dutch capture slave-trading fort of Elmina, Ghana.
1641	Frederick Henry's son, William, marries Mary, daughter of Charles I of England.
1647	William II succeeds Frederick Henry.
1648	Treaty of Münster recognises Dutch independence.

The Dutch Republic

1650	William dies; first stadholderless period, except in Friesland and Groningen.
1652	Jan van Riebeeck establishes settlement at Cape of Good Hope.
1652-4	First Anglo-Dutch naval war.
1653	Johan de Witt, Grand Pensionary of Holland.
1661	Dutch capture Ceylon.
1664	English seize New Amsterdam (New York).
1665-7	Second Anglo-Dutch War; Dutch attack on Medway.
1668	Triple Alliance between Dutch Republic, England and Sweden.
1670	Secret treaty between Charles II and Louis XIV for attack on Dutch.
1672	Third Anglo-Dutch War; French invasion; de Witt murdered by mob; William III stadholder.
1674	Charles II makes peace.
1677	William III marries Mary, daughter of James, Duke of York.
1678	Treaty of Nijmegen ends war with France.
1688	Louis XIV declares war on Netherlands; Whigs offer William English crown.
1689	William and Mary joint monarchs of England.
1697	Treaty of Rijswijk ends war with France.
1702	William dies; second stadholderless period.
1747	French invasion during War of Austrian Succession; William IV stadholder.
1766	William V.
1780-4	Fourth Anglo-Dutch War.
1785-7	Patriot revolt.
1787	Prussian troops restore William V.
1795	French invasion; end of Dutch republic; Batavian republic.

French Occupation

1798	Directory of Five.
1805	Schimmelpenninck Grand Pensionary.
1806	Louis Napoleon King of Holland.
1810	Louis abdicates; Netherlands part of French empire.
1813	French troops start evacuation; William I, stadholder's son, returns.

The Kingdom of the Netherlands

1815	Belgium made part of the Netherlands.
1824	King's personal rule in East Indies.
1825-30	Javanese revolt.
1830	Belgian revolt.
1838	Forced labour system in Java.
1839	Netherlands acknowledges Belgian independence.
1840	William I abdicates; William II succeeds.
1848	Constitution revised.
1853	Catholic emancipation.
1870	Forced labour abolished in Java, except for coffee.
1874	First factory law.
1876	North Sea Canal to Amsterdam.
1878	Anti-Revolutionary Party formed —first modern political party.
1890	Royal Dutch Petroleum Company.
1891	Philips factory at Eindhoven.
1892	Strict Calvinists form Reformed Church.
1898	First Hague peace conference
1900	Compulsory education.
1901	Social insurance and industrial accidents insurance.
1903	Railway and dock strike in Amsterdam.
1914	Dutch neutral in First World War.
1916	Extensive flooding.
1917-9	Universal suffrage; proportional representation; subsidies for for denominational schools.
1919	KLM formed.
1920	Zuider Zee works start.
1922	Constitutional reform in East Indies.
1926	Uprising in East Indies suppressed.
1940	German invasion; Rotterdam bombed; German occupation.
1944	Arnhem airborne landing.
1947	Benelux formed.
1949	Indonesia independent.
1950	Social-Economic Council, representing government, employers and unions, formed.

1953	Floods in South Holland and Zeeland; Delta plan.
1954	Charter for Kingdom makes Netherlands Surinam and Antilles equal partners.
1962	Natural gas discovered in Groningen.
1963	Netherlands New Guinea province becomes part of Indonesia as West Irian.
1964	Provo movement.
1966	Crown Princess Beatrix marries German Claus von Amsberg; new party, Democracy '66.
1968	Secondary education act; Pastoral Council, including laymen, to advise Catholic hierarchy.
1971	University reforms admit students to governing bodies.
1972	Voting age reduced to 18.
1974	Hague conference proposes full independence for Surinam and Netherlands Antilles.
1975	November last date for Surinamese to take Dutch citizenship.

The Stadholder

The stadholder, originally a lieutenant-governor representing the Burgundian and Habsburg rulers, became a symbol of national unity when Prince William of Orange (known as the Silent) led the revolt against Spain in the sixteenth century. After the breach with Spain, stadholders continued to be appointed by the provincial governments. There was usually one main stadholder for the five provinces of Holland, Zeeland, Utrecht, Gelderland and Overijssel and another for Friesland and Groningen in the north.

The stadholders had some of the powers and much of the prestige of a monarch, but they were dependent on the support of the provinces. There were frequent quarrels between the stadholders and the most powerful province of Holland. As a result there were two periods when no main stadholder was appointed, 1650-72 and 1702-47.

With the appointment of William IV in 1747, the office was made hereditary in all seven provinces of the Dutch republic, cementing the relationship between the House of Orange and the Netherlands, which has continued uninterrupted into the present kingdom.

Kings and Queens

1815-40	William I (abdicated).
1840-9	William II.
1849-90	William III.
1890-8	Queen Emma (regent).
1898-1948	Queen Wilhelmina (abdicated).
1948-	Queen Juliana.

The Arts

VISUAL ARTS

Hieronymus Bosch (c. 1450-1516) master of fantasy and allegorical paintings, *The Temptation of St. Anthony, The Hay Wain.*

Lucas van Leyden (1494-1533), portraits, religious paintings, engravings.

Abraham Bloemaert (1564-1651) historical, genre paintings, founded Utrecht school.

Frans Hals (1581/5-1666), portraits, *The Laughing Cavalier, St. George's Guild Banquet.*

Hendrick Terbrugghen (1588-1629) genre, religious paintings.

Gerrit van Honthorst (1590-1656) biblical and genre painter, chiaroscuro technique.

Jan van Goyen (1596-1656) prolific landscape painter.

Rembrandt van Rijn (1606-69) greatest Dutch painter, etcher, *The Night Watch, Anatomy Lesson of Dr. Tulp,* self-portraits.

Adriaen van Ostade (1610-84) painter of peasants.

Willem van de Velde (1611-93) and his son Willem (1633-1707) marine artists in London.

Gerrit Dou (1613-75) precise, detailed portrait and genre painter.

Bartholomeus van der Helst (1613-70), portraits, *Banquet of The Amsterdam Civic Guard,* rated higher than Rembrandt by Sir Joshua Reynolds.

Gerard Ter Borch (1617-81) precocious portraitist, *Peace of Münster.*

Aelbert Cuyp (1620-91) versatile painter of landscapes, townscapes, portraits, still life.

Paulus Potter (1625-54) animal painter/etcher, *Young Bull.*

Jan Steen (c. 1626-79) tavern scenes.

Jacob van Ruisdael (1628/9-82) landscapes, *The Windmill at Wijk.*

Pieter de Hooch (1629-83?) domestic scenes, *Courtyard, The Pantry.*

Jan Vermeer (1632-75) genre, *A Woman at the Virginals, View of Delft.*

Meindert Hobbema (1638-1709) last great landscape painter of Golden Age, *The Avenue at Middelharnis.*

Rachel Ruysch (1664-1750) flower pieces, still lifes.

Jan van Huysum (1682-1749) greatest Dutch flower painter.

Cornelis Troost (1697-1750) painter/print maker, genre, conversation pieces, sometimes called Dutch Hogarth.

Jozef Israels (1824-1911) realistic paintings of everyday life, Hague school.

Johan Barthold Jongkind (1819-91) landscapes, etchings, worked in France, precursor of impressionism.

Vincent Willem van Gogh (1853-90) swirling brush strokes, vivid colours, worked mainly in France. *Self Portrait, Yellow Cornfield.*

Jan Theodoor Toorop (1858-1928) symbolist, *Trio Fleuri.*

Piet Mondriaan (1872-1944) abstract, co-founder of *De Stijl. Trees.*

Maurits Cornelis Escher (1898-1972) graphic artist, complex fantasies.

Willem de Kooning (1904-) abstract expressionist, naturalised American.

Constant (Constant A. Nieuwenhys) (1920-) Cobra group, designs and models for ideal city, *New Babylon.*

Karel Appel (1921-) abstract expressionist, action painter.

Co Westerik (1924-) modern realist, anticipated pop art.

LITERATURE

Desiderius Erasmus (1466/9-1536) scholar, humanist, *The Praise of Folly.*

Jacob Cats (1577-1660) 'Father' Cats, best-selling moralising verses, *The Mirror of Old and New Times.*

Hugo de Groot (Grotius) (1583-1645) founder of international law, *On the Law of War and Peace,* also poet, playwright.

Pieter Cornelisz. Hooft (1581-1647) historian, poet, playwright. Castle at Muiden an intellectual centre.

Joost van den Vondel (1587-1679) greatest Dutch poet, dramatist, trilogy of *Lucifer, Adam in Exile* and *Noah.*

Constantijn Huygens (1596-1687) witty, sophisticated poet and satirist, translated John Donne.

Gysbert Japicx (1603-66) founder of modern Frisian language, poet.

Justus van Effen (1684-1735) *De Hollandsche Spectator,* modelled on Addison, reintroduced use of Dutch in place of fashionable French in literature.

Elisabeth Wolff-Bekker (1738-1804) and **Agatha Deken** (1741-1804) novels in letter-form, *Sara Burgerhart, Willem Leevend.*

Edward Douwes Dekker (1820-87) pseudonym Multatuli, attacked Dutch colonial policy in *Max Havelaar.*

Louis Couperus (1863-1923) realistic novelist, *Old People and the Things that Pass.*

Simon Vestdijk (1898-1971) prolific novelist, essayist, poet.

Willem Frederik Hermans (1921-) powerful novelist, *The Dark Room of Damocles.*

Gerard Kornelis van het Reve (1923-) controversial novelist, *The Evenings.*

Harry Mulisch (1927-) novels, short stories, reportage on Eichmann trial and Provo movement.

Reference
The Economy

The Economy

Since the end of the Second World War, the
Dutch economy has been booming.
Rotterdam has become the biggest port in
the world. Almost half of the country's
energy is supplied by the vast supplies of
natural gas. Agriculture has been
rationalised. Industry has expanded rapidly.

In spite of worldwide economic
problems, there was still a modest growth
rate of 2 per cent in 1974 and inflation was
contained at just under 10 per cent.
Natural gas cushioned the effects of
increases in oil prices, so that the
Netherlands continued to have a healthy
balance of payments surplus. The guilder
is among the strongest E.E.C. currencies.

But there are some serious underlying
problems. Exports account for nearly half
of the gnp. The Netherlands is particularly
susceptible to any recession in trade,
especially with West Germany, by far the
biggest trading partner. At home, the
failure to control wages, produced fears
about the competitiveness of exports.
Unemployment has been rising rapidly. It
stood at 1·4 per cent in December, 1970, and
had reached 4·5 per cent in January, 1975.
There is also a structural imbalance in the
economy, with too much industry
concentrated in the west.

58

Agriculture in the Netherlands

- Wheat
- Oats
- Barley
- Sugar Beet
- Potatoes
- Market Gardening
- Bulbs
- Orchard Fruits
- Dairy Products
- Cattle
- Pigs
- Principal Fishing Ports

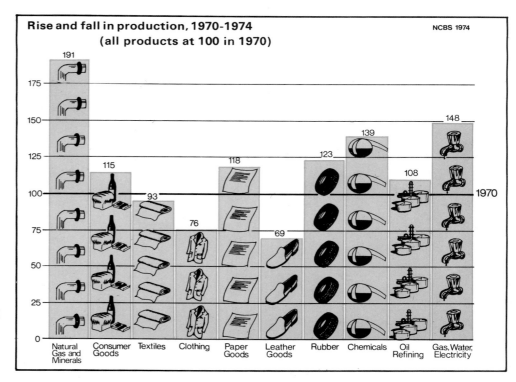

Rise and fall in production, 1970-1974
(all products at 100 in 1970)

NCBS 1974

Natural Gas and Minerals	Consumer Goods	Textiles	Clothing	Paper Goods	Leather Goods	Rubber	Chemicals	Oil Refining	Gas, Water, Electricity
191	115	93	76	118	69	123	139	108	148

1970

Labour

NCBS 1974

Employed population: 4,793,000

Agriculture and Fisheries 304,000

1,611,000 Industry and Building

Services, Trade and Catering 2,116,000

619,000 Public Sector: Civil Service and local Government

8,684,000

Non-Working Population

143,000 Unemployed

Industry in the Netherlands

◇ Principal Coalmining Areas
■ Iron & Steel
◆ Natural Gas
Common Salt
Major Industrial Centres
Mechanical Engineering
Electrical Engineering
Shipbuilding
Motor Vehicles
Rubber Products

▲ Chemicals
Oilfields
Oil Refineries
Textiles Districts

Leeuwarden
Groningen
Haarlem
Amsterdam
Hilversum
Apeldoorn
Enschede
's Gravenhage (The Hague)
Utrecht
Arnhem
Rotterdam
Dordrecht
Breda
Tilburg
Eindhoven

Paper
Precision Instruments
Leather Goods
Shoes
Glass
Pottery
Sugar Refineries
Tobacco Manufacturing
Breweries
Diamond Polishing

Imports and exports

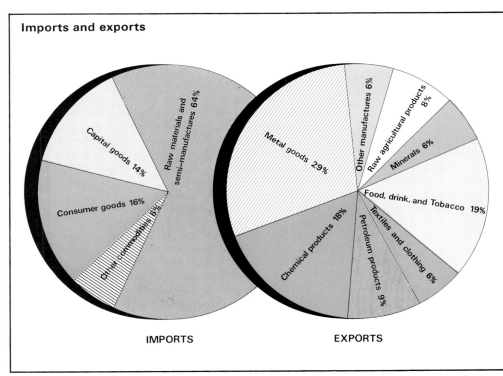

Raw materials and semi-manufactures 64%
Capital goods 14%
Consumer goods 16%
Other commodities 6%

IMPORTS

Metal goods 29%
Other manufactures 6%
Raw agricultural products 8%
Minerals 6%
Food, drink, and Tobacco 19%
Textiles and clothing 6%
Petroleum products 9%
Chemical products 18%

EXPORTS

Principal trade partners

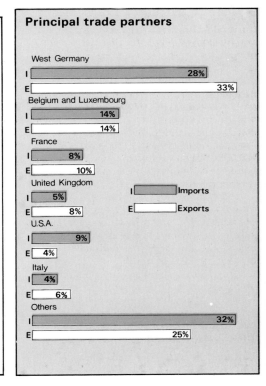

West Germany
I 28%
E 33%

Belgium and Luxembourg
I 14%
E 14%

France
I 8%
E 10%

United Kingdom
I 5%
E 8%

U.S.A.
I 9%
E 4%

Italy
I 4%
E 6%

Others
I 32%
E 25%

I Imports
E Exports

Gazetteer

Alkmaar (52 38N 4 44E) North Holland. Historic canal town. An important vegetable and dairy products centre, famous for its open-air cheese market.

Amersfoort (52 09N 5 23E) Medieval town centre with former priory and water gates. Horticultural and poultry centre and light industries. Pop (1973) 79,876.

Amsterdam (52 21N 4 54E) North Holland, capital of country. Big inland port linked to North Sea and Rhine by canals. Financial, banking and cultural centre. Diamonds, beer, ship-building, engineering, chemicals. Seven thousand protected buildings, including Rembrandt's house. Two universities—Municipal and Free. Pop. (1973) 1,018,641.

Apeldoorn (52 13N 5 57E) Gelderland. Health centre near forests and hills. Het Loo, Queen Wilhelmina's palace after her abdication. Manufactures paper products and pharmaceuticals. Pop. (1973) 128,610.

Arnhem (52 00N 5 53E) capital of Gelderland. Made famous by Allied airborne landing in September, 1944. Tourist centre. Mixed industries. Pop. (1973) 276,985.

Breda (51 35N 4 46E) North Brabant. Scene of much fighting in Eighty Years' War. Catholic centre. 1531 beguinage occupied by original order. Food processing and machinery manufacture. Pop. (1973) 151,162.

Delft (52 01N 4 21E) South Holland. Canal town, where William the Silent was assassinated. Dutch monarchs buried in New Church. Famous for Delftware (glazed earthenware). Birthplace of Jan Vermeer. Pop. (1973) 87,571.

Delfzijl (53 19N 6 56E) Groningen. Rapidly growing industrial area, based on natural gas.

Delta region, South Holland and Zeeland. Huge project to block off estuaries of great rivers to prevent flooding. Western Scheldt and New Waterway will remain open for access to Antwerp and Rotterdam respectively.

Den Helder (52·54N 4·45E) at northern tip of North Holland. Main naval base. Pop. (1973) 61,457.

Dordrecht (51 48N 4 40E) South Holland, popularly known as Dort. First important port and shipbuilding centre in the country. Shipbuilding, metallurgical and chemical industries. Pop. (1973) 177,879.

Eindhoven (51 26N 5 30E) North Brabant. Developed as major industrial centre from founding of Philips' electrical factory in 1891. Also manufactures cars, textiles, tobacco products. Pop. (1973) 347,717.

Enschede (52 13N 6 55E) Overijssel. Main textile centre, rebuilt after Second World War. Twente University of Technology. Pop. (1973) 238,296.

Frisian Islands off northern coast separated from mainland by Wadden Sea. Five main islands, Texel, Vlieland, Terschelling, Ameland and Schiermonnikoog. Popular holiday resorts.

Geleen (50 58N 5 52E) centre of big chemicals industry, based on pipelines bringing in natural gas from Groningen and petroleum by-products from Rotterdam. Pop. (1973) 37,050.

Gouda (52 01N 4 43E) South Holland. Typical old merchants' town with famous cheese market. Pop. (1973) 47,920.

Groningen (53 13N 6 35E) capital of its province. Important northern trade centre for agriculture and industries. Second oldest university, founded 1614. Pop. (1973) 205,880.

Haarlem (52 23N 4 38E) capital of North Holland. Centre for bulb trade. Frans Hals museum. Historic buildings. Pop. (1973) 237,991.

Hague, The (52 05N 4 16E) called 's-Gravenhage or Den Haag. Seat of government and diplomatic centre. Much splendid architecture, including the thirteenth-century Binnenhof. Increasing industrial development on outskirts. Pop. (1973) 693,890.

Heerlen (50 53N 5 59E) Limburg. Former coal mining area. Most pits now closed. Pop. (1973) 265,280.

's-Hertogenbosch (51 41N 5 19E) or **Den Bosch,** capital of North Brabant. Fine medieval buildings, including Gothic St. Janskerk. Pop. (1973) 173,114.

Hilversum (52 14N 5 10E) North Holland. Radio and television centre. Pop. (1973) 113,273.

Hoge Veluwe (52 02N 5 55E) National Park which also contains the Kröller-Müller Museum of modern sculpture and painting.

IJmuiden (52 28N 4 38E) North Sea port linked to Amsterdam by North Sea Canal. Important fishing port.

IJsselmeer (52 45N 5 25E) freshwater lake of 120,000 hectares, created out of former Zuider Zee.

Leeuwarden (53 12N 5 48E) capital of Friesland. Cattle and food-processing centre. Pop. (1973) 86,339.

Leiden (52 10N 4 30E) South Holland. Famous university town with many historic buildings and museums. Important textile centre from fifteenth to eighteenth centuries. Bulb-growing centre. Birthplace of Rembrandt and asylum for Pilgrim Fathers. Pop. (1973) 164,887.

Lelystad (52 31N 5 27E) newest town in country, built on land reclaimed from former Zuider Zee. Named after C. Lely who planned the reclamation scheme.

Maas (51 49N 5 01E) or Meuse, important river, 950 km. long, rising in France and flowing through Belgium and the Netherlands. One branch flows into the Hollandsch Diep, the other into the Waal.

Maastricht (50 51N 5 42E) capital of Limburg. Ancient Roman town with many medieval buildings. Wide range of manufactures, including paper and chemicals. Growing tourist centre, convenient for Germany and Belgium. Pop. (1973) 145,277.

Middelburg (51 30N 3 36E) capital of Zeeland. Flooded during Second World War, but many ancient monuments restored. Tourist centre. Metal and textile industries.

Nijmegen (51 50N 5 52E) Gelderland. Roman settlement. Imperial residence in Carolingian times. Important industrial centre for metal, machinery, paper, artificial fibres and clothing. Roman Catholic university. Pop. (1973) 209,164.

Polder region, north-east of Amsterdam, formed out of Zuider Zee. It contains five large areas of reclaimed land: Wieringermeer polder (20,000 hectares); Noordoostpolder (48,000 hectares); Oostelijk Flevoland (54,000 hectares); Zuidelijk Flevoland (43 000 hectares); and Markerwaard (60,000 hectares). The last is due to be completed in 1980.

Rhine (51 52N 6 02E) major European river, 1,320 km. long, rising in Alps, with its estuary in the Netherlands, where it divides into the IJssel, the Lek and the Waal. It has been one of the major sources of the Netherlands trading prosperity for many centuries.

Randstad, or rim town, the horseshoe-shaped conurbation in the west, which contains many of the major cities, including Amsterdam, Haarlem, Leiden, The Hague, Delft, Rotterdam and Dordrecht.

Rotterdam (51 55N 4 28E) biggest port in the Netherlands, handling more tonnage than any port in the world. Linked to North Sea by New Waterway. New Europoort handles super-tankers. Rebuilt after being bombed by Germans in Second World War with Lijnbaan shopping precinct and de Doelen concert hall and conference centre. Big commercial centre. Pop. (1973) 1,055,157.

Scheveningen (52 05N 4 16E) fishing port and popular seaside resort near The Hague.

Schelde, or **Scheldt.** river, 435km. long, rising in France and flowing through Belgium, but with its outlet to the sea in the Netherlands.

Soestdijk (52 12N 5 15E), village near Hilversum, containing Queen's palace.

Tilburg (51 34N 5 05E) North Brabant. Developed in last century into one of main industrial centres with textiles and light industries. Pop. (1973) 210,535.

Utrecht (52 06N 5 07E) capital of its province. Seat of important Catholic principality in Middle Ages, now seat of Dutch primate. Railway headquarters and diversified industrial base. State university, founded 1636. (Pop. (1973) 464,053.

Vlissingen (51 27N 3 35E), or Flushing, on Walcheren island in Zeeland. Flooded in Second World War and in 1953. Shipbuilding port and holiday resort. Pop. (1973) 42,639.

Zaandam (52 26N 4 49E) industrial centre. Museum of windmills. Pop. (1973) 136,435.

Zandvoort (52 22N 4 32E) Seaside resort near Haarlem. Grand Prix motor circuit.

Zutphen (52 08N 6 12E) Gelderland. Ancient Hanseatic town with medieval fortifications. Timber trade, paper and textile industries.

Zwolle (52 31N 6 06E) capital of Overijssel. Agricultural and industrial centre. Pop. (1973) 77,122.

Index

Numbers in **heavy** type refer to illustrations

Agriculture 38
Allotments **15**
Amsterdam **14**, 17, 21, 22, 23, 26, 30, **30**, 34, **34**, 40, 42, 43, 45, 46, 47, **52**
Amsterdam Concertgebouw Orchestra **40**
Antique shops 30
Architecture 24

Baking school **19**
Baltic 10, 26
Bargaining 30, 50
Barges 14, **15**, **42**
Barrel organs **47**
Beatrix, Princess **36**, 48
Begijnhof **35**
Belgium 29, 44
Bernhard, Prince Consort **36**, 48
Bicycles 42, **43**
Binnenhof 36, **36**
Bird sanctuaries 40
Birthdays 14, 46
Black Piet 46
Blankers-Koen, Fanny 28
Boers 13
Bourgeois society 12, 51
Brabant 47
Bric-a-brac **47**
Brielle 20, **26**
Britain 45

Calvinism 16, 17
Canals 10, **11**, **19**, 28, 34, **35**, 36, 40, 42, 43
Cape of Good Hope **13**
Carnegie, Andrew 23
Catholicism 16, 17, 22, 52
Charles II of England 12
Cheese market **39**
Claus, Prince 48
Clogs **31**, **46-47**
Cruyff, Johan 28, **29**
Curaçao 12
Cuyp, Aelbert 24
Cycling 28, **29**

Daf car plant **38**
Dairy farming 38
Day and Night **25**
Decimal system 13
Delfshaven **23**
Delft 20, 30
Delta project 32, 53
Denominational schools 18
Descartes, René 23
Diamonds **38-39**
Dikes 10, **10**, 20
Docker, The **21**

Dodge, Mary Mapes 48
Drucker, Wilhelmina 52

E.E.C. 26, 27, 38, 42
East India Company 26
Eighty Years War 17, 20, 22, 26
Eindhoven 38, **52**
Eleven Towns Race **28**
England 20, 26
Erasmus 23, **49**
Escher, M.C. 25
Explorers 12

Family 14, **15**, 46
Fens, in East Anglia 12
First World War 18, 38
Fishing 26, **29**, 40
Flea markets 31
Flower market **39**
Fluyt 26
Flying Dutchman, The **49**
Football 28
France 9, 23
Frank, Anne 23
French invasion, 1795 **21**
Friesland **9**, 10, 28, 40, **41**, 47
Friesian cattle 38, **38**

Gaper **45**
Genre painting 24
Gérard, Balthasar 20
Germany 9, 22, 38, 44, 52
Gheyn, Jacob de 20
Gouda 39
Grandfather clock 12, **13**
Groningen 38
Grotius, Hugo **22**

Haarlem, lake **10**, **15**
Hague, The 17, 23, 30, 36, **36**, 40, 41, 47
Hall of Knights 36, **36**
Hals, Franz 24
Herengracht 34
"Hero of Haarlem" **48**
Het Dorp 53
Heyn, Piet 48
Hilversum 45
Holland 9, 15, 36, 38
Holland Festival 40
Hooch, Pieter de 24
Huguenots 23
Huygens, Christiaan **13**
Hydraulic engineering 12

Ice-skating 28, **40**
Indonesia 32, 52
Industry 38, 52
Inquisition 20
International Court of Justice 23
International law 22

Java 26
Jews 22, 23
Juliana, Queen 36, **36**, **37**

K.L.M. Airline 42, 43
Kabouters **21**, 52
Kenwood House, London 25

Keukenhof 40, 51
Knitting **18**

Lakes 10, 28, 29, 40
Languages, facility in 44
Leeghwater, Jan Adriaanszoon **10**
Leeuwarden 28
Leeuwenhoek, Antony van **13**
Leiden 20, 23, 40
Leiden University **19**
Limburg 8, 16, **41**
Lisse 40
Locke, John 23

Maas **8**, **9**, 10
"Mad Minnies" **52**
Madurodam **41**
Margarine 32
Marine charts 26
Market stalls 30, **31**
Maurice, Prince of Orange 20
Medway, Dutch attack on **20**
Microscope **13**
Middleburg 17, **25**
Middle Ages 9, 26, 34
Mint Tower **35**
Mondriaan, Piet 24
Monument for a Devastated City 22
Mud-walking **41**
Music 24, 40
Musketeers **20**

N.O.S. 45
Natural gas 38
Nature reserves 40
Navigation 13
New Zealand **27**
Noise, complaints of 14
North Brabant 8, 16
North Holland 31, 39
North Sea 9, 26, 40, 42, 44
Nuns 17

Olympic Games 28
Orange-Nassau, House of 48

Painters 12, 24
Peace Palace, The Hague **23**
Peeters, Jan 20
Peter the Great 12
Philip II of Spain 20
Philips 38, 52
Pilgrim Fathers 23
Poland 22
Polders **11**, 38
Pottery 30
Priests, marriage of 17
Prinsengracht 34
Protestantism 16, 17, 20, 52

Queen Juliana, ferry-boat **27**

Reclaimed land **11**, 12, 34, **53**
Reformed Church 16
Refugees 22
Regional costume 40, **46**
Rembrandt 24, 25
Rhine 8, 10
Riebeeck, Jan van **13**
Rijsttafel 32, **32**
Rijksdaalder **30**

Rotterdam 22, 26, 27, 38, **39**, **42**, 47, 49
Royal Netherlands F.A. 28
Royal Palace, Dam Square 34, **34**
Royal Standard **36**
Ruska, Wim 28
Ruyter, Michael de 48, **49**

Scheldt 8, 10
Schenk, Ard 28
Scheveningen 40
Schipol Airport 34, **43**
Sea Beggars 20, **26**
Seamen 12, 26, 27
Second World War 21, 23, 34
Shell 38
Soestdijk **36**, **46**
South Africa 12, **13**
South Holland 9, **11**, 39, 40
Spaarndam 48
Spain 9, 12, 16, 20, 22, 26, 40
Spinoza, Baruch 23
Spionnetje **50**
Spring cleaning **51**
St. Nicholas 46, **49**
Staphorst **16**, 46
Stellendam **11**
Stevin, Simon **13**
Strike, 1941 21
Supreme Court of Justice **36**

Tasmania **27**
Telescope 13
Television 44, 45
Tiles, glazed **12**
Trade 8, 10, 26
Tramcars 43, **45**
Trekschuiten **42**
Tromp, Maarten Harpertszoon **26**
Tulips **12**, **26**, 40, 51

"Underground" radio 21
Unilever 38

Valkenburg **41**
Van Gogh, Vincent 24
Vermeer 24
Verzuiling 17
Veseler, Joris 45
Volendam 17, 46
Volvo 38
Vondel, Joost van den 24

Wadden Sea **41**
Waffenhandlung 20
Waghenaer, Lucas van 26
West Germany 28
Wilhelmina, Queen 48
Willaert, Adriaan 24
William II, King 36
William II, Count of Holland 36
William the Silent 20, **20**, 36, **48**
Windmills 8, 10, **10**, **11**, **12**
Woman and Maid in a Courtyard **24**
Women and civil rights 52

Yachting 12, 28, **29**

Zeeland 9, **11**, **17**, 46, 49
Zuider Zee 9, 53

1 2 3 4 5 6 7 8 9 10-CAD-81 80 79 78 77

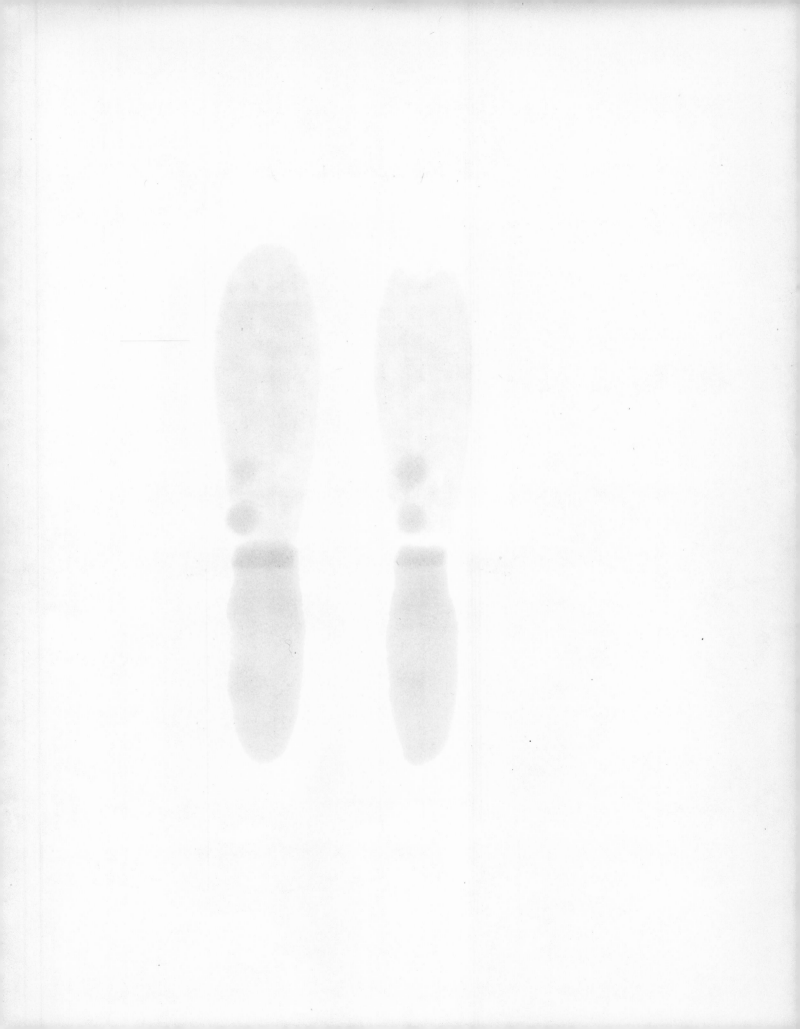

le

DATE DUE		
FEB 21 1986		
Plessien		